W9-DBW-517

Adolescence

Life-Span Human Development Series

Series Editors: Freda Rebelsky, Boston University, and Lynn Dorman

Infancy
Kathryn Sherrod, George Peabody College for Teachers
Peter Vietze, National Institutes of Health
Steven Friedman

Early Childhood
Donald L. Peters, The Pennsylvania State University
Sherry L. Willis, The Pennsylvania State University

The Middle Years of Childhood
Patricia Minuchin, Temple University

Adolescence
Kathleen M. White, Boston University
Joseph C. Speisman, Boston University

Early and Middle Adulthood
Lillian E. Troll, Rutgers University

Late Adulthood: Perspectives on Human Development
Richard A. Kalish, Berkeley, California

Cross-Cultural Human Development
Robert L. Munroe, Pitzer College
Ruth H. Munroe, Pitzer College

Life-Span Developmental Psychology:
Introduction to Research Methods
Paul B. Baltes, The Pennsylvania State University
Hayne W. Reese, West Virginia University
John R. Nesselroade, The Pennsylvania State University

Biological Perspectives in Developmental Psychology
George F. Michel, Boston University
Celia L. Moore, University of Massachusetts

Cognitive Development: A Life-Span View
George E. Forman, University of Massachusetts
Irving E. Sigel, Educational Testing Service

Personality Development through the Life Span
Barbara M. Newman, Ohio State University
Philip R. Newman

Adolescence

Kathleen M. White
Joseph C. Speisman

Boston University

BROOKS/COLE PUBLISHING COMPANY
MONTEREY, CALIFORNIA
A Division of Wadsworth Publishing Company, Inc.

To Richard and Berta, and our friend Caroline Fish Murray

Printed in the United States of America

10 9 8 7 6 5

Library of Congress Cataloging in Publication Data

White, Kathleen, 1940-
  Adolescence.

  (Life-span human development series)
  Bibliography: p.
  Includes index.
  1. Adolescent psychology. I. Speisman, Joseph Chester, 1924-   joint author.   II. Title.
BF724.W43   155.5   76-26158
ISBN 0-8185-0205-3

Manuscript Editor: *Linda Hansen*
Production Editor: *Joan Marsh*
Cover Design: *John Edeen*
Interior Design: *Linda Marcetti*

Series Foreword

What are the changes we see over the life span? How can we explain them? And how do we account for individual differences? The Life-Span Human Development Series provides a new way to look at these questions. It approaches human development from three major perspectives: (1) a focus on basic issues related to the study of life-span developmental psychology, such as methodology and research design, cross-cultural and longitudinal studies, age-stage phenomena, and stability and change; (2) a focus on age divisions—infancy, early childhood, middle childhood, adolescence, young and middle adulthood, and late adulthood; and (3) a focus on developmental areas such as physiology, cognition, language, perception, sex roles, and personality.

There is some overlap in the content of these volumes. We believe that it will be stimulating to the reader to think the same idea through from the viewpoints of different authors or from the viewpoints of different areas of development. For example, language development is the subject of one volume and is also discussed in the volume on cross-cultural development, among others.

Instructors and students may use the entire series for a thorough survey of life-span developmental psychology or, since each volume can be used independently, may choose selected volumes to cover specific concept areas or age ranges. Volumes that focus on basic issues can be used to introduce the student to the life-span concept.

No single author could adequately cover the entire field as we have defined it. Our authors found it exciting to focus on their areas of specialization within a limited space while, at the same time, expanding their thinking to encompass the entire life span. It can be beneficial to both author and student to attempt a new integration of familiar material. Since we think it also benefits students to see ideas in development, we encouraged the authors not only to review the relevant literature but also to use what they now know to point up possible new areas of study. As a result, the student will learn to think about human development rather than just learn the facts of development.

Freda Rebelsky
Lynn Dorman

Preface

This is a book with a point of view. Unlike the typical omnibus adolescent text, it is not a compendium. We have not tried to summarize the thousands of investigations devoted to adolescents. Instead, we have taken the views of two principal theorists on adolescence, Erikson and Piaget, and have examined their insights into social-emotional and cognitive (intellectual) development. We *have* reviewed much of the research in the more traditional areas such as physical development, sex-role development, moral development, peer interactions, and family relationships. However, we have considered these findings largely within a framework that emphasizes qualitative changes in the individual's way of thinking, types of interactions, and personal identity. We also have emphasized sexual development and moral development—areas that, we think, illustrate how changes in thinking and in relationships combine to make the adolescent very different from the younger child.

We also have initiated an exploration of the adaptive, functional meaning of an adolescent period for cultures or civilizations. We do not believe that adolescence is a universal phenomenon. We do believe that an adolescent period of development becomes essential as societies become more complex. We consider the cognitive and social-emotional changes that occur during adolescence to be vital to an understanding of the changes that take place in complex, industrial (largely Western) societies. Much of our focus, therefore, has been on the Western, and particularly on the North American, adolescent. While we have been somewhat selective about the evidence presented, we have tried to be sufficiently comprehensive so as to enable students to reach an informed position on the issues that is either in agreement or disagreement with our own view.

Several times in the past few years, we have asked each college student enrolled in a course on postchildhood development to submit an anonymous autobiographical essay describing his or her own adolescence that focused on when it began, when (and if) it ended, what the major concerns were, what relationships were important, and how concerns and relationships changed and developed. Students responded to this request with openness and with remarkable self-disclosure. In order to illustrate and breathe life into the issues under discussion, we will use excerpts from these autobiographies throughout this book. Although our purpose is not to "prove" anything about adolescence, some of the autobiographical statements highlight exactly those characteristics that we think are crucial to a definition of adolescence.

Many of our colleagues and students have been helpful reviewers of preliminary drafts of the manuscript. Our thanks go to Marjorie Withers, Patricia Daniel, Jane Snyder, Jessica Phillips, Annette Ferstenberg, Elinor Macy, George Michel, Celia Moore, Augusto Blasi, Fred Elmadjian, and Nina Fish Murray. Erich Labouvie of the University of Wisconsin and L. Eugene Thomas of the University of Connecticut also provided helpful reviews of the manuscript. We also want to thank the series editors, Freda Rebelsky and Lynn Dorman, as well as our Brooks/Cole editor, Todd Lueders, for their support and their encouragement, and most of all for their criticism.

Kathleen M. White
Joseph C. Speisman

Contents

Chapter One

Adolescents: Who or What Are They?

Mine was an easy adolescence. Most growth came so gradually it was hardly noticeable. The only thing that changed was my view of myself. I used to fantasize becoming beautiful, brilliant and popular. I still have fantasies but now I'm myself in them.

I developed very fast. Needing a bra at 10 really embarrassed me. I did everything to hide it.

As for my self-concept, I felt different from everyone else. I never joined cliques and didn't have many good friends. I felt ridiculed but enjoyed feeling like a martyr. I loved hating people and did things deliberately to get them to make fun of me.

I hated school and its injustices. I sulked through every class. I hated Sunday School for the same reason. It was the same kind of blind authority we were supposed to obey even though the teachers were 50 times stupider than we.

As for my family, I was very close to them. They were a refuge. I never felt any need to rebel.

What is adolescence? Is it a time of conflict, rebellion, distress, and generation gaps? Is it a time of amazed and joyous self-awareness? Is it a time of quiet introspection? Or are these the wrong questions to ask? The purpose of this chapter is to explore the kinds of questions that are useful, and to discover those questions that are not useful, in trying to understand what makes adolescence a significant time. Indeed, we believe that the existence of an adolescent period is as important to the growth of humankind as it is to the growth of the individual. In cultures in which there is no adolescent period there is little change over the years, either in individuals or in the societies to which they belong.

Psychologists who work with disturbed youth portray adolescence as a difficult period. Anna Freud (1966) emphasizes the "incomprehensible and irreconcilable contradictions" of adolescence.

> Adolescents are excessively egoistic, regarding themselves as the center of the universe and the sole object of interest, and yet at no time in later life are they capable of so much self-sacrifice and devotion. They form the most passionate love relations, only to break them off as abruptly as they began them. . . . They oscillate between blind submission to some self-chosen leader and defiant rebellion against any and every authority. They are selfish and materially minded and at the same time full of lofty idealism. . . .Their moods veer between light-hearted optimism and the blackest pessimism [pp. 137–138].

Anna Freud's view of adolescence seems quite consistent with the portrait of youth countercultures and student radicals that is sometimes popularized by the media. It is not, however, an unchallenged view. It currently is fashionable among many psychologists to reject the assumption that adolescence is a period of rebellion or emotional confusion. Gold and Douvan (1969, p. 3) ask "Where are the tensions, the crises, the muddled, befuddled, struggling, exasperating personalities, lurching spasmodically through the teen years? When we contemplate the systematic empirical literature, we find that adolescents really don't go through all that." Thornburg (1971, p. 3), after reviewing much of the same empirical literature, reaches a different conclusion: "Although we no longer accept Hall's (1904) storm-and-stress . . . theory that adolescence is an inevitable period of emotional conflict, we cannot deny that today's youth are highly conflict oriented." Kohlberg and Gilligan (1971) see adolescence at the very least as a period of "heightened emotionality."

The issues of how stressful adolescence is and of how rebellious adolescents are, are popular ones, and seem to have intrinsic interest for many people. Yet the main concern should not be with whether or not adolescence is *stressful*, which is partly a matter of definition. The questions are why, under what circumstances, in which individuals, and with what implications is adolescence stressful? The Group for the Advancement of Psychiatry (1968) argues that if adolescence is stressful, it is not because of biological changes, which are universal, but because of particular kinds of pressures and demands on the adolescent, which vary cross-culturally. Implicit in this view is the notion that adolescence may be more stressful in some groups and for some individuals than for others. What is still needed, however, is a truly developmental perspective, a perspective that helps us understand what it is about adolescents that leads many of them, at their particular stage in life, to experience stress in the face of certain demands and pressures.

We will return frequently to the question of what constitutes a "truly developmental perspective," but we would like to raise several questions here. What, if anything, makes adolescence a unique time? If adolescence does prove to be stormy for some individuals, what is the cause? Is adolescence just an age span—roughly the teen years—or are there more helpful criteria for defining it?

Unfortunately, it is not possible to answer any of these questions simply by reviewing the empirical literature. L'Abaté (1971, p. 201) reports that between 1927 and 1966 there were a total of 3283 publications dealing with adolescence. This is a substantial base, quantitatively, for inference. These publications cover a wide range of topics: peer relationships, family interactions, academic performance, sexual identification, personality development, and so on. However, in relation to any particular issue, such as "storm and stress" for example, the findings are frequently contradictory, often trivial, and certainly subject to varying interpretations. Such studies provide much descriptive information about many different samplings of teenagers. What they do not provide is an adequate framework for understanding these differing descriptions.

Asking adolescents or postadolescents about their experiences, like reading empirical literature, cannot provide definitive answers as to the nature and significance of adolescence. It can, however, provide a dramatic picture of how certain aspects of life are experienced by individual adolescents. Descriptions of adolescence can be examined from at least three different perspectives: (1) the *content* (concerns, issues) of adolescent experience, (2) the *structures* (ways of knowing) that adolescents bring to their experience, and (3) the *function* of an adolescent period for society. These three perspectives indicate different approaches toward defining adolescence.

It is clear, in looking at adolescence from the perspective of *content,* that there are a number of issues that confront adolescents. There is, for example, individuation, especially as it pertains to the individual's increasing independence from the family; there are also occupational choice, sexuality, and the acquisition of a set of principles by which to live. All of these concerns are involved in the construct that Erikson calls "identity." As you will see in Chapter Four, for many adolescents these challenges constitute an identity crisis that can be resolved in a number of different ways. Some adolescents work through the crisis and achieve a sense of personal identity. For others, the whole attempt breaks down into identity diffusion or role confusion; this is commonly known as "alienation." Whether or not an adolescent achieves a sense of identity, such issues frequently become crucial for the first time during the teen years, and teenagers generally must deal with them in some way, even if only by avoiding them. However, identity issues are by no means confined to the teens. From the point of view of content, then, adolescence is a distinct stage in identity or personality development. It is characterized by concerns which are different from those of earlier stages of life and which shape, to some extent, the concerns of the future, such as of rearing a family of one's own. One college man summarizes his adolescent years thusly:

> It was a lot of good times—good friends, good family life, and a time for getting to know a little bit more about who I was, am, becoming. It was a time of challenge—a time when everything I had previously accepted must be challenged, including myself. Values, ideas, concepts had to be worked out and had to be mine—had to be accepted by me as complementary to the basic "I." I feel that most of the anxiety and frustration normally associated with those years actually refers to this challenge. It is a process that begins and ends with the deepest, most secretive introspection. It is a process of growth that continues throughout life—and, quite frankly, I see nothing so terrible, nothing so awkward in those adolescent years. After all, I survived, didn't I?

When the perspective shifts from the issues *about* which adolescents think to *how* they think about these issues, it is a *structural* perspective. As you will see, adolescents are not at all homogeneous when it comes to structure. For example, adolescents who can solve scientific problems only in a concrete, trial-and-error way are using qualitatively different cognitive structures than adolescents who can manipulate abstractions mentally and solve problems systematically. Adolescents who say all premarital sex is bad, because it just "isn't nice" and "it will make their parents unhappy," are functioning at a qualitatively different stage of moral judgment than adolescents who say that right now sex "isn't right for them" because they are not yet sure enough of themselves and their ability to make commitments. A college woman, taking another perspective, says:

> The boys we dated were usually a couple years older than us. We were aware of our sexuality and talked an awful lot about sex, but always on a hypothetical level. We never indulged in anything "heavy"—not like the kids today. It is hard to look back and write this because at that time—say five or six years ago, dating, college, and everyday problems were huge crises—and now they do not seem to be as important as they once were. But no one could have convinced me of that way back then. I thought that what I was going through was unique and special to me.

The kind of structural growth that takes place in some young people over the course of their adolescence is illustrated in the following quote. Note that the issues which concerned this young woman remained somewhat stable, but the way in which she thought about them changed. It is these ways of thinking that reflect her cognitive structures.

> In religion class, we debated the morality of many things, like church attendance, civil disobedience, premarital intercourse, marriages outside the faith, cheating in school, the Vietnam war. The so-called smart kids usually started the discussions, but as a member of that caste, I believe we were the most successfully socialized members of the school. What we thought was right was usually the opinion of the teacher or adults in general. Although we were taught "Thou shalt not kill," at first none of us questioned the morality of the war, because the nuns didn't. Being against the war was not socially accepted. It took me a long time to speak against anything—the pressures of conformity were very strong. It wasn't until I took a job and began making friends with public school kids that my conscience developed into a cause of behavior.

This young woman's reminiscences seem to reflect progress during her teens from one stage of thinking about moral problems to another. As we will see in Chapter Three, the age at which a given adolescent reaches a particular *stage of thinking* varies, as indeed does the likelihood of the individual ever achieving certain higher levels of thinking. Cognitive psychologists, using a structural perspective, would not call adolescence a distinct stage of cognitive development because, although two teenagers may be the same age and may grapple with the same problems, they may approach those problems with qualitatively different types of thinking. A structural perspective allows us to speak of cognitive stages or moral judgment stages and to characterize adolescent thought according to the stage of cognitive or moral development that it reflects. Certain types of thinking—that is, certain cognitive structures characteristic of certain stages—are unlikely to emerge before adolescence, and are likely to be achieved after puberty, given certain experiences in a technological society. Nevertheless, from a structural perspective, this overlap of stage with age does not justify calling the adolescent period a cognitive developmental stage.

The third perspective focuses on the *function* of adolescence both in the life of the individual and in the development of society. From this point of view, the principal question to be asked is what function (purpose, outcome) is served by the nature of the transition between childhood and adulthood. This transition differs cross-culturally both in duration and in the continuity or discontinuity it provides for past roles and expectations. Even while asserting that adolescence is not universally stressful, Margaret Mead (1974, p. 52) holds that in primitive societies, as well as among the modern urban and rural poor, individuals move from childhood into early adolescence and then *immediately* into adulthood—after which they age early. Clearly what she is calling adolescence in these particular circumstances is highly attenuated and restricted in opportunity, compared to adolescence as we generally conceive of it. In fact, some psychologists, for example, Bernard (1971), would argue that at least in primitive societies there is *no* adolescence at all. A comparison of teenage individuals in the above-mentioned groups to teenagers in middle-class North America is actually a comparison of teenage adults to teenage adolescents rather than a comparison of two adolescent groups.

There is considerable agreement (Bakan, 1971; Elkind, 1971; Mead, 1974) that adolescence as we know it—that is, a prolonged period of transition between childhood and adulthood, widely available to the members of society—is a modern invention. Moreover, there is considerable agreement (Benedict, 1938; Hsu, 1961) that during this prolonged transition the individual frequently is faced with new sets of roles and expectations that are *discontinuous* with previous roles and expectations. For example, adolescents, in contrast to children, are expected to be more responsible and to become more dominant in relations with others. Older adolescents are expected to become well adjusted sexual partners, even though up to this point sex has been taboo (Benedict, 1938).

Finally, there is widespread agreement (Eisenberg, 1965; Erikson, 1968; Hsu, 1961; Mead, 1974; Piaget, 1968) that adolescence is a prolonged, not necessarily smooth, transitional period that makes possible a literate and technologically advanced society. Civilization advances because humans, with their unique cognitive capacities, undergo an extended training experience that permits them to acquire some of the skills, knowledge, and wisdom of the past in order to build on these for the future.

What are the kinds of developments that allow individuals to become philosophers, scientists, inventors, artists, and managers? We are interested in what contributes to a sense of ethics and the acquisition of human virtues in a technological society—a process that may be very different from that in a simple society in which there may not even be words for hate or war. A simple society may boast great warriors, hunters, composers of song, weavers of rugs, and accomplishments that the world-weary of our own society would like to recapture; it does not need ethical philosophers, scientists, or social critics, because the established ways of doing things are in some sense good enough.

In rapidly changing societies it is the existence of, and developments during, the adolescent period that allows humans to examine where they are—and should be—going. In a changing society, the side effects of adolescent development often may seem unsettling to those adults who are concerned with stability. As one man observes: "I see no hope for the future of our people if they are dependent on the frivolous youths of today, for certainly all youth are reckless beyond words. . . . When I was a boy, we were taught to be discreet and respectful of elders, but the present youth are exceedingly wise and impatient of restraint."

Whose words are these? Your father's? Your friend's father's? One of our fathers'? No, that was Hesiod speaking in the eighth century B.C. What did the youth of whom he spoke have in common with many of today's youth? They had democracy, a republic, a period of time between childhood and the assumption of adult responsibilities, the perception of alternative ways of doing things, and, perhaps most important, the experience of some *choice* in what they were to be.

Chapter Two

Toward an Integrated View of Adolescence

Erikson and Piaget

The Men and Their Theories

Our readers may agree with this book's deductive approach of proceeding from theory to data. Still, readers might wonder why we have chosen to follow the theories of Erikson and Piaget. We will try to answer that question by presenting some of their basic theoretical concepts. In later sections of the chapter we will review Piaget's and Erikson's descriptions of the stages before adolescence as well as of adolescence itself.

The value of integrating Piaget's and Erikson's theories stems partly from their consideration, in human development, of what Piaget has called "two sides of the same coin": the cognitive (intellectual) and the affective (emotional) aspects of development. Piaget has examined in great depth the evolution of intelligence in humans. His concern has been with qualitative changes in cognitive functioning in the course of development. Erikson has considered in equal depth the evolution of personality and emotions in humans. His concern has been with qualitative changes in personality in the course of development. Both Piaget and Erikson hold that cognitive and emotional development are in reality intertwined and inseparable, but each man has chosen to focus primarily on just one area. Moreover, in their different emphases, Piaget has developed a structural theory, and Erikson has described the content of the adolescent period.

We believe that the theories formulated by Piaget and Erikson are the most helpful tools available for understanding human development. It has been Erikson's contention that to understand a point of view, one must know the personal and historical context in which it arose. We agree wholeheartedly with this assertion. Just as disparate data make most sense in the context of a unifying and organizing theory, theories make most sense in the context of a personal and social history. In the same way, knowledge about Piaget's and Erikson's personal development can help in understanding their theories. There is nothing mysterious in their choosing to study different areas of human development. Their life histories are in many ways also different. Let's turn first to Erikson's background and key concepts, and then examine Piaget's background and views.

Erik Erikson, who gave us the term *identity crisis,* knew firsthand what an identity crisis was all about.[1] As a youngster, Erikson was not a good student. He disliked the strictness and formality of school, which he attended until the age of 18. After graduating from high school, he spent seven years drifting around Europe, sometimes studying art, generally reading widely, and always trying to find himself. He seemed to be granting himself what he later was to call an extended *psychosocial moratorium,* a "breathing period" during which he could establish his identity.

At the age of 25, Erikson gave up his wandering—but not yet his intention to be a children's portrait artist—to join with Peter Blos in operating a small, private, "progressive" school for children whose parents were in analysis with Freud or one of Freud's followers. As was fashionable with the intellectual community in Vienna at that time, Erikson himself entered analysis upon the invitation of his friend, Anna Freud. While continuing to teach and to paint portraits of children, Erikson also embarked on clinical training in child analysis. A love of children and a concern for their healthy development has been one of his life's themes.

Erikson finished his analytic training in 1933 at the age of 31—just in time to flee from an increasingly violent Europe as Hitler rose to power. He traveled to the United States, where he practiced psychoanalysis and held clinical and teaching appointments at Harvard, Yale, and Berkeley. He also did field work with several tribes of American Indians, counseled World War II veterans, and began a residential treatment program for disturbed adolescents in Stockbridge, Massachusetts.

As one result of his diverse clinical endeavors, Erikson coined the term *identity crisis* to refer to the alienation from both self and society that he observed in disturbed Indians, veterans, and adolescents, and also, to a less serious degree, in normal adolescents.

What are some of the key concepts in the theory of this artist-teacher-psychoanalyst? Erikson (1968) views human growth in terms of conflicts, inner and outer. Each individual must weather successive *psychosocial crises,* which represent conflicts between the demands of the social environment and biological or psychological needs and drives. Development involves inter-

---

[1] For more complete biographical details, see Coles (1970), the principal source for the biographical material included here.

actions with an ever-widening circle of significant individuals and institutions. During these interactions the developing individual progressively gains active mastery of the environment, personality integration, and accurate perception of self and world. All these occur if the environment helps the individual to master the crises in a progressive rather than a regressive way.

Erikson—who, as has been mentioned, spent many years searching for and developing his own identity—gives the concept of identity a key role in his theory of psychosocial development. While the identity crisis is the defining issue of the adolescent years, it has its foundations in all earlier psychosocial crises and provides a basis for all later ones. If the early social environment of the child is hostile or unduly restrictive, or if adolescents are not allowed a psychosocial moratorium to "find themselves," then society and the individual both will bear the cost in lost productivity. Erikson was granted a moratorium to wander and search, and he and the world have profited from his clinical and literary productivity.

If Erikson represents the alienated youth, the artist, the soul-searcher, and the radical educator, Piaget represents the precocious scholar, the determined scientist, the coolly logical philosopher.[2] Piaget's first publication, a description of an albino sparrow, was published in a natural history magazine when he was only 11 years old. When he was 15, he published a paper on molluscs that resulted in his being offered the post of mollusc curator at the Geneva museum of natural history. He declined the offer in order to finish high school.

Piaget's early interest in the natural sciences was climaxed by his completion of a Ph.D. in biology at the age of 22. Also during his adolescent years he was becoming increasingly intrigued by epistemology, or the study of knowledge. He grappled with such epistemological questions as: What is knowledge? How is it acquired? What is the relationship between the knower and the known? His approach to these questions developed during what seems to have been a psychosocial moratorium. From the ages of 15 to 20, he experienced a crisis around the conflict between his religious upbringing and his new commitment to science. At the age of 20, he took a year off from his studies to recover from "nervous exhaustion" in the Swiss Alps. During that year he wrote a novel, *Recherche,* which explored many of the philosophical questions he has spent his life pursuing (Gardner, 1972, pp. 53–54).

At the age of 22, when Piaget had completed his doctorate and published his novel, he had not yet formulated a completely satisfactory life plan. He wanted to continue his work in the natural sciences without sacrificing his interest in philosophy, but he was not sure how to combine these endeavors. He spent some time working in a psychoanalytic clinic, and then in a

[2]For additional biographical and theoretical detail, see Ginsburg and Opper (1969) and Gardner (1972).

psychological clinic, and finally took a position in the Binet laboratory in Paris helping standardize an intelligence test. It was then that he became convinced that scientific answers to his epistemological questions were possible. That is, he became convinced that, to understand what knowing is, one must look at how the child goes about knowing things and at the different ways in which children know things at different ages.

What are some of the key concepts in the theory of this biologist-philosopher, this genetic epistemologist? According to Piaget, intelligence is understood best as an evolutionary, biological achievement that allows the individual to interact effectively with the environment. Intellectual development cannot be explained solely in terms of maturation, learning, or social transmission of knowledge. Rather, like other biological achievements, it is characterized by progressive changes in a process of active adaptation. Like other biological processes, it facilitates a balance, or "dynamic equilibrium," between the individual and the environment.

In Piaget's view, intelligence must be characterized in terms of both process and structure. Intelligence as a process is characterized at all ages by its organization and adaptability. Intelligence as structure means that it changes with the individual's interaction with the environment. The infant is born with very few reflex structures, but, as a result of interaction with the environment, these structures become progressively differentiated and integrated. As part of the adaptive process, the child *assimilates* new experience to existing structures and *accommodates* (modifies) existing structures on the basis of this new experience. As a result of this process, cognitive development proceeds in an invariant sequence through a series of qualitatively different stages, each stage organized and adaptive but progressing toward higher levels of equilibrium between individual and environment.

While it is possible to view Erikson's developmental theory as a psychosocial view of personality and Piaget's theory as a biological view of intelligence, the two share important structural elements and philosophical notions. These similarities probably are related to the cultural and philosophical milieu in which Erikson and Piaget were educated. Both theories have their roots in what Allport (1957) has called the European—as opposed to Anglo-American—philosophical tradition. Because the congruences between Piagetian and Eriksonian theories are at least as important as their differences, we would like to describe briefly the philosophical tradition that they share, and its contrast with the Anglo-American perspective.

Anglo-American and European theories differ in their views of, for example, the whole and its parts, the nature of mental life, and the concern with methodology (Allport, 1957). Briefly, the development of theories seems to have been carried on largely by European thinkers, while Anglo-American psychologists have been more concerned with experimental design, statistical tests, methodology, and the empirical results of experimental work.

European theories have tended to focus on the "whole person," while Anglo-American theories have been more likely to focus on discrete parts, such as response, factor (a statistical concept), and attitude. Moreover, English and North American psychologists have tended to look at the mind or intellect as a blank slate, which is written on by experience. This is a tradition that goes back to John Locke's (1632–1704) *Treatise on Human Understanding*. In this view, humans are seen as reactive beings, reacting to and being shaped totally by environmental events. European psychologists, by contrast, have tended to look at the human intellect as self-active. In their view, humans are neither blank slates, nor simply reactive beings. Instead, they are born with distinctively human needs and characteristics, and actively seek interaction with and satisfaction from their environment.

Falling clearly into the European philosophical perspective, Erikson and Piaget have been criticized by Anglo-American psychologists for a lack of experimental rigor. Such psychologists challenge the construction of elaborate theories on the basis of limited empirical findings that possibly are derived from biased samples. Despite these criticisms, it is questionable whether any North American or British psychologists have built a system that has as much explanatory utility as Erikson's or Piaget's.

Erikson and Piaget also fall into the European tradition of concern with the whole person. Neither is interested in studying behavior—either its acquisition or its performance—per se. Behavior is of interest to them only insofar as it contributes to the understanding of the human animal and to the ways in which humans are able to interact with their environment. Additionally, behavior is never viewed by them simply as a response to environmental input; rather, behavior reflects the active efforts of the individual to structure and interpret the environment.

Piaget and Erikson thus share an interest in theory-building, a focus on the whole person, and a view of humans as self-motivated and active beings. Their theories also share an "epigenetic" model of development, that is, a model that characterizes growth as being organized into qualitatively distinct stages that represent the outcome of interactions between individuals and their environment. These important interrelated concepts of epigenesis, stages, and interaction underlie Piaget's and Erikson's descriptions of characteristic behaviors of children and adolescents and will be discussed in later sections of the chapter.

Epigenesis, Stage, and Interaction

Piaget and Erikson borrow the term "epigenesis" from biology. In biology, epigenesis means the development of an embryo from a more-or-less structureless cell as a result of the interaction of the environment and the protoplasm. Epigenesis stands in opposition to the traditional nature-nurture, heredity-environment dualism and emphasizes instead an interaction between organism and environment in all development.

Piaget (1970) believes that, like embryological development, cognitive development involves a process of construction in which the structure originally supplied by heredity is progressively modified as a result of the organism's active involvement with its environment. Thus, logic is not an innate human gift that simply ripens with maturity, but an epigenetic construction. Maturation opens up possibilities for the emergence of new cognitive structures. In order for these possibilities to become realities, the individual must engage in social interactions and appropriate physical and intellectual activities.

Erikson sees embryological development as providing a useful analogy for personality development. He points out that during the prenatal period each organ and body part has its time of origin. If something disturbs the proper rate and normal sequence of development, body parts in their critical period of emergence will never develop normally, as illustrated by the tragedy of the thalidomide babies. After birth, Erikson holds, the epigenetic principle creates a succession of potentialities for interaction between the individual and others.

What does Erikson mean by "potentialities for interaction"? In essence, he argues that there is an important relationship between the child's developing capabilities and concerns and society's ability to offer widening opportunities for growth and experience. When babies are most helpless, dependent, and unknowing, they must be cared for and protected completely. As they gain control over language and locomotion they need an opportunity to explore, to ask questions, to meet new people, and to see new things. As they achieve physical and intellectual maturity during adolescence, they must be permitted to establish an identity and life of their own, apart from their families.

Piaget and Erikson both emphasize *stages* in epigenetic development that involve fundamental changes in modes of interacting with the environment. Piaget's notion of stage is built on a notion of cognitive *structures.* He holds that each stage is characterized by the appearance of new structures that build upon and incorporate earlier ones. Cognitive structures are the tools by which individuals know and interact with their environment. Infants are born with reflex structures such as sucking and looking: they know the world largely through the mouth and eyes. After infancy, children develop structures that allow them to classify and seriate objects: they know the world largely through their concrete experience of it. Adolescents develop structures that allow them to deal with total abstractions: they know the world as one expression of a series of possibilities (including utopias).

In Piaget's theory, each individual's interactions with the environment are given lip service as the means by which structures develop and change. In Erikson's system, the emphasis is on the content of those inter-actions. Erikson has no concept of structure comparable to Piaget's. What seems to develop through stages in Erikson's system are the individual's dispositions to act and feel in certain ways: to trust or mistrust, to exercise initiative, or to feel shame. It may be that the same underlying cognitive structures make possible both the cognitive interactions on which Piaget focuses and the social and emotional interactions on which Erikson focuses. Or it may be that the social and emotional interactions observed by Erikson contribute to the structural changes observed by Piaget. David Elkind, a Piagetian scholar, argues that the cognitive structures peculiar to any given age period can provide insight into the personality characteristics of that age level (1971, p. 50). Erikson, taking a somewhat different perspective, suggests that intellectual functioning during each psychosocial stage is either integrated with or distorted by emotional striving.

In the next section, we will explore cognitive and emotional develop-ment before adolescence. We will try to show how progress in earlier stages paves the way for mature identity and formal logic—the achievements of adolescence. Although it will not be possible to conclude that intellectual structures cause psychosocial crises—or vice versa—the relationships be-tween intellectual and psychosocial development should become clearer. Our portrait of the developing individual is drawn directly from the theoretical formulations of Erikson and Piaget.

Foundations of Adolescence

Infancy

Erikson and Piaget agree that infancy is a crucial period of develop-ment. Psychosocially, the first year of life is a critical period for the emergence of a sense of trust or of mistrust. With the mouth as the focal point of existence, infants learn something about the world into which they are born—whether it is warm or cold, loving or hostile, caring or neglecting.

The sense of trust that the psychologically healthy infant develops becomes the cornerstone of the evolving personality. By contrast, the child who fails to develop a healthy sense of trust may be plagued by emotional in-security and the inability to establish an identity during adolescence. The absence of a sense of mutual support and love in infancy can endanger the adolescent identity process, making individuals fearful of leaving childhood behind and of putting trust in their own independent movement into adult-hood (Erikson, 1968, p. 105).

A "sense of trust" presupposes someone to trust and, ultimately, presupposes that there is a world, apart from the self, to be trusted. Yet newborn babies appear to be unable to differentiate between themselves and others and, indeed, show no awareness of where they stop and the rest of the world begins. The infant is in this sense egocentric (without ego or identity) since at first there seems to be neither self nor other for the infant. The beginnings of identity take form during infancy, as babies differentiate between themselves and others and achieve some recognition of the permanence of objects.

Piaget believes that, for all practical purposes, infants construct their own universe and differentiate themselves from it. Through the physical manipulations of themselves and objects, through the playing with toys and practicing of skills, and through the psychological activities corresponding to all these, babies evolve from being individuals largely dependent on reflexes and parental benevolence to being individuals who can use means to accomplish ends, have awareness of the permanence of objects, imitate novel actions either immediately or in deferred fashion, and show comprehension of certain aspects of time, space, and causality. This *sensorimotor stage* of "practical" intelligence is the foundation for all later psychological development (Piaget, 1968, p. 9).

Early Childhood

Knowing by doing and interrelating with the world give way to more sophisticated kinds of interactions. The child's social and emotional interactions during very early childhood, particularly in the second year of life, focus on the eliminative organs—hence Freud's "anal period." Consistent with his interactionist framework, Erikson holds that the ease or difficulty of the psychosocial crisis surrounding toilet training depends on whether or not the culture attaches importance to it (1968, p. 107). In our Western society, excessive parental concern with cleanliness and punctuality may make early childhood a trying time and may produce compulsivity. The whole stage becomes a battle for autonomy, who will decide whose body is going to do what, when, and in which place. If children are allowed to develop in self-control and self-esteem, they are left with a lasting sense of free will. If they are subject to strong parental control and are frightened at their own loss of self-control, they may be left with a lasting sense of doubt and shame. In adolescence, such individuals may go through the identity crisis feeling ashamed, apologetic, and afraid to be seen, or they may overcompensate with defiant participation in a gang (Erikson, 1968, p. 111).

Psychosocially, early childhood can be characterized by the emergence of the child's sense of autonomy. Cognitively, it is characterized by the emergence of the symbolic function. During the *preoperational phase* (around 1½ to 4 years of age), cognition is transformed from a sensorimotor, or practical, intelligence to the beginnings of real thought. It is during these preoperational years that the child develops the ability to make one thing, such as a word or an object, represent something else. For example, a child can symbolically represent a dog with the word "dog," a loud "Bow-wow!" sound, a toy dog, a mitten, a box, or anything else an evolving imagination permits. Similarly, a shoe thrown in the toilet by a child can represent either feces or the body, as the child seeks to determine what kinds of things can be flushed away, and what cannot.

After acquiring language, children become increasingly involved with the social world and the world of inner representation. Language facilitates and widens the scope of communication, thus contributing to the socialization of the child. In an expanding environment, children, through mental representation, learn to deal with objects even when they are not present. A child at this stage can, for example, use symbolic play to adjust better to the realities of mother-child relationships by manipulating mother and baby dolls in a variety of situations. The expression of frustrations centering around toilet training are just one type of event exercising the emerging symbolic function. Many psychologists argue that it is language, or the symbolic function, that is the most important achievement of humans.

Preschool Age

What follows the emergence of the symbolic function and the establishment of a sense of autonomy? The preschool years (4 to 6 years of age) are a play age, a time of anticipation of roles. In this, the Oedipal stage, the little girl plays at being a woman and dreams of being married to her daddy—as well as of being a tennis player or a dancer. The little boy plays at being a man and dreams of being married to his mommy—as well as of being a teacher or a bus driver.

The psychosocial crisis of the Oedipal stage involves initiative versus guilt. Along with developing language and locomotion and being stimulated by curiosity and imagination, children begin to develop a conscience. If the incipient superego is overburdened by severe and excessively moralistic parents, the child may develop long-lasting resentments. One of the deepest conflicts in life may focus on hate for parents who served initially as models for the conscience but who later were found performing the very actions that adolescents learned not to tolerate in themselves (Erikson, 1968, p. 119).

While Erikson views the Oedipal (phallic) years as a separate and important developmental stage, Piaget sees them as an extension of the preoperational period. Thus, these preschool years are not characterized by the emergence of any new cognitive structures. The child's thinking is becoming more organized and conceptual but is not yet truly logical.

In the intuitive phase (approximately 4 to 6 years of age) of *pre-operational thought*, reasoning is dominated by perceptual effects and an inability to consider more than one attribute of things at a time. For example, a child may be able to count two rows of five tokens each (that takes organization) but may think that one row has more tokens because it is more spread out (that involves domination by perceptual effects). Or, a child may divide shapes into separate groups of squares and circles (that takes a conceptual orientation) but may tell you that there are more squares than shapes (that involves an inability to consider more than one attribute—shapeness and squareness—at a time).

During the preschool years, moral feelings become attached to parent-child interactions (Piaget, 1968, p. 37). These first moral feelings, like early thought, are intuitive rather than mature. Early moral values are rigid and inflexible. They are objective rules obeyed by the child because of uni-lateral respect for the parents. To some extent this rigid blame- and punish-ment-oriented conscience of the preschool child seems to be a developmental phenomenon independent of the particular punitiveness of the parents. That is, early conscience reflects immaturity in cognitive development more than it reflects any particular pattern of child-rearing. While Erikson's clinical ob-servations may help us understand the lasting resentment of the youth who bears the burden of an overly strict superego, Piaget's data help us understand the built-in limitations of early moral judgment.

School Age

What further cognitive and personality developments take place before adolescence? What Freud calls the latency period (approximately 6 or 7 to 11 years of age) seems to be a decisive stage socially. During these school-age years the child may gain a lasting sense of industry or of inferiority. As children encounter both the promise and the demands of schoolwork, there is the sense of preparation for the future world of work and career. With exposure to broader social values, children acquire either a feeling of participation or of exclusion on the basis of such characteristics as color, sex, or ethnic background. If children leave this preadolescent stage with a sense of inferiority, then it becomes doubly difficult for them to establish a sense of identity during adolescence.

The elementary school years constitute a stage of critical importance for cognitive development also. It is during this *concrete operational stage* that a true logic, tied to concrete objects, emerges. The development of new mental structures and new mental operations allows the child to overcome the limitations of intuitive thought. For example, if children around the age of 5 see juice poured from one glass into a taller and narrower glass, they will say either that there is now more juice (because the height has increased) or less juice (because the width has decreased). They do not yet have the operation of reversibility, that is, the mental activity of returning the juice to its original state. They focus on states rather than on transformations. If children around the age of 7 are faced with the same problem, they are not fooled by its perceptual pull. They will say that the amount of juice is the same because "you only poured it," or "it's taller now, but it's skinnier too and so it's still the same." They have developed the ability to *conserve* the amount of the substance despite superficial changes in the perceptual attributes of the substance. According to Piaget, the child between the ages of 6 and 11 develops conservation of such concrete characteristics of objects as number, length, mass, weight, and volume.

The cognitive abilities emerging during the concrete operational stage affect the child's social life also. Piaget notes that, after the age of 7, children become capable of cooperation because they no longer confuse their own point of view with that of others. Children become capable of true discussions—of real importance in adolescence—rather than collective monologues. They understand that games are played by rules for the good of the players and that the rules are invented by people. As children become increasingly capable of a real morality, as opposed to simple obedience, exclusion on the basis of characteristics such as race may only heighten their sense of inferiority and contribute to the later difficulty of establishing a sense of identity.

The synthesis of cognitive and psychosocial developmental theories that we have just presented fills a long-recognized gap in the understanding of the "whole child." Flavell, for example, has argued that a knowledge of Piaget's work significantly enriches Erikson's account of the affective (emotional) and interpersonal life of the child. Flavell summarizes nicely the kind of integration that can be made:

> Using the adolescent or adult as a standard of comparison, it can be said with confidence that the five-year-old simply does not have the *conceptual* wherewithall to worry much about the world situation, plan for his future, or experience the delights and agonies of an adult love relationship [Flavell, 1963, p. 42, italics added].

The next section will consider the adolescent as the "standard of comparison" developing beyond the achievements of childhood. Again, our consideration of cognitive and psychosocial development will be a synthesis of the views of Erikson and Piaget.

Adolescence

pre adolescence

We have seen that the social foundations of adolescence lie in an expanding series of interactions that leave the individual with a sense of trust or mistrust, autonomy or doubt, initiative or guilt, and industriousness or inferiority. The cognitive foundations of adolescence lie in an expanding series of interactions that allow the individual to adapt to an ever-widening reality, first based solely on action, later with rigid and prelogical internal representations, and finally with reversible concrete operations. What new potentials and achievements become possible in adolescence?

Certainly puberty signals the achievement of genital maturity and the potential for adult sexuality and procreation. However, as noted in Chapter One, adolescence represents much more than the attainment of puberty. Sexual maturation may contribute to the emotional tone of adolescence; however, in accounting for the developments of adolescence, pubertal changes seem secondary to changes in thought and emotion (Piaget, 1969, p. 60). Moreover, while psychoanalysis has emphasized genitality as a prerequisite for full maturity, a truly loving and intimate sexual relationship presupposes the establishment of a firm identity during adolescence (Erikson, 1968, pp. 136–137). Thus, it is important to look at social and psychological as well as biological changes if we are to have a complete and useful picture of human development.

Piaget and Erikson both examine the intellectual and emotional achievements of adolescence that lead to adult responsibilities. Both are interested in the broadening of a time perspective and the role of peer interactions in contributing to the adolescent's progress. Both pinpoint preparation for adult social and occupational roles as the tasks to which adolescence is committed. Finally, both are interested in the ways in which particular environments either foster and support, or inhibit and deny, adolescent potential.

According to Piaget, the adolescent, in contrast to the child, is an individual who can construct systems and theories. Children can think about objects, their classes, relations, numbers, and characteristics. Adolescents can think about thought. They can reflect on the operation of their own cognitive processes. They can reason on the basis of the purely hypothetical. They can—and frequently do—conceive abstract theories about politics, utopia, and love. They can construct whole new worlds, peopled by loving human beings, in their minds. In keeping with an epigenetic perspective, the transition from concrete to *formal operations, or to hypothetical-deductive thinking, is a "fundamental transformation"* (Piaget, 1968, p. 61). It is a transformation involving a shift of logical operations from a level of concrete manipulation to a level where they are free of all perceptual, experiential, or other support. The ability to think in terms of the purely hypothetical is a powerful tool in the adolescent's attempt to establish an identity. An orientation toward the realm of the possible aids the adolescent in choosing personal, occupational, sexual, and ideological commitments (Erikson, 1968, p. 245). That is, it allows young people to consider alternative models of what they would like to become. The preadolescent child may fantasize about becoming a cowboy or a policeman, without any understanding of the requirements or implications of these roles. The adolescent becomes aware of a broader range of occupational choices and begins thinking about their appropriateness to personal needs and interests. Adolescents also begin to conceive of themselves as potential mates, parents, and community members. Their search for identity may become most problematical when the widest range of possible alternatives can be envisioned (Erikson, 1968, p. 245).

Young people may be overwhelmed by the onslaught of conflicting possibilities and choices (Erikson, 1968, p. 133). This source of frustration may be aggravated by another, opposing, source: just when the adolescent's conception of roles is expanding, society, with narrower opportunities, is countering many possibilities. While adolescents are telling themselves they can be anything they want to be, society is telling them, in very different terms, what they must do and who they must be if they are to succeed or even to survive. Just when their thought broadens to include new perspectives and expectations, reality narrows the choice.

One important component of the youth's blossoming cognitive development is the articulation of a time perspective. The ability to think beyond the present is one of the most important achievements differentiating adolescents from children (Inhelder & Piaget, 1958). As part of this developing time perspective, many young European people formulate a *life plan* (Piaget, 1968). In their life plans, adolescents elaborate their intentions for personal and social change, or even revolution. They outline their ideas for the world of tomorrow and their own role in it. They project an image of themselves as the same essential beings but better, wiser, more successful, and more deserving of the praise and admiration of others.

The formulation of a life plan may be an attempt to deal with the discomfort of an evolving *historical perspective*. This new perspective involves "a sense of the irreversibility of significant events and an often urgent need to understand fully and quickly what kinds of happenings in reality and in thought determine others, and why" (Erikson, 1968, p. 247). As adolescents become capable of understanding the extent to which they are products of their own families and their own history, it becomes important to them to prove that they have identities of their own. Much of adolescent "rebellion" may be an effort to stake out a claim for self-determination. Life plans thus may be a way of saying "I will be what I want to be, not what you made me."

Does the adolescent's cognitive blossoming, ability to conceive different role possibilities, and expanding time perspective mean that childhood modes of thinking and interacting are lost forever? No. In their epigenetic frameworks, Piaget and Erikson allow for a sort of "recapitulation" of earlier problems and achievements at a new level.

The beginning of every cognitive stage is characterized by egocentricity—that is, a failure to distinguish between self and other, a confusion of subjective and objective. This egocentrism takes different forms at different stages. At the same time that small infants are gaining some sensorimotor control over experience, their actions demonstrate that they are unable to differentiate between their own bodies and the rest of the world. At the same time that young children are gaining some control over language as a communicative tool, they show that they are unable to distinguish between their own view and that of others. Finally, at the same time that adolescents are mastering the ability to deal with the purely hypothetical, they demonstrate their belief in the omnipotence of their own thinking. That is, they subordinate the real to the possible, acting "as though the world should submit itself to idealistic schemes rather than to systems of reality" (Piaget, 1968, p. 64).

Adolescent cognitive egocentrism seems to be intricately bound up in an emotional concern with social roles. Adolescents try not only to adapt themselves to the social environment but also to adapt the environment to themselves (Inhelder & Piaget, 1958, p. 343). Giddy with new intellectual powers, young people conceive the transformation of the world with Messianic fervor. In words not unlike those of Anna Freud (p. 2), Piaget observes that "the adolescent's systems or life plans are at the same time filled with generous sentiments and altruistic or mystically fervent projects and with disquieting megalomania and conscious egocentricity" (1968, p. 66). This kind of internal disquiet is not confined to the neurotic or anxious youngster but is a potential *inherent in* the intellectual developments of adolescence.

Adolescence is also a time for the recapitulation and integration of components of identity achieved in earlier stages. Just as infants must learn to trust themselves and others, adolescents must find ideas and individuals in whom to have faith. Just as toddlers must experience and assert their own autonomy, adolescents insist on the right to decide on their future by their own free will. Just as preschoolers exercise their imagination in playing at all the things they might be, adolescents are committed to attaining a role worthy of their ambitions. Finally, just as school age children are concerned with performing tasks well, adolescents are determined to find a career from which they can derive a sense of satisfaction.

How do adolescents overcome their egocentricity? How do they integrate the different components of their identities? One important avenue is their interactions with their peers. Piaget views the overcoming of ego-centrism as a *decentering* process. This decentering, or shift from a more limited to a more differentiated viewpoint, always takes place simultaneously in thought processes and in social relationships. The tendency of adolescents to form closely knit peer groups is not just the effect of pressures toward conformity but is also indispensable to decentering. Individuals try out their theories and discover their weaknesses by sharing ideas with peers. Individual Messianism may blend into general agreement as to the absolute necessity of social reform and subordination of the self to a larger activist involvement (Piaget, 1968, p. 68). Discussion is the key to this process and is the goal of adolescent social interaction. Discussion is a means of combatting the "real world" and reconstructing it in common with others.

Psychosocially, the chief task of adolescence is not only to con-solidate one's identity but also to establish a commitment, deserving one's utmost fidelity, to society and the future. One way of formulating identity is by trying out various roles with friends, seeing which ones are confirmed and comfortable. Even "young love" is a part of this process. That is, youthful romances may involve a great deal of conversation simply because it is through conversation that boys and girls project a self-image and see it reflected and clarified in the eyes of their love.

Youthful romances also may involve a good deal of mental playing with the possible. That is, adolescent love may encompass the projection of an ideal onto a real being. The discovery of the discrepancy between the ideal and the real can account for the disappointments that are so typical of young love (Piaget, 1968, p. 67). Caught up in their own imaginative processes, adolescents may view their affairs of the heart as though they were occurring in a novel. This dramatic concern with their own love stories could affect adolescents more strongly than any instinctual sex drives (Piaget, 1968, pp. 67–68).

The climax of adolescent development comes with the young person's commitment to a vocation. It is likely that any remaining cognitive egocentricity, any continuing tendency to confuse the real with the possible, is overcome when adolescents begin a real job or at least undertake serious professional training (Inhelder & Piaget, 1958, p. 346).[3] Moreover, a vocation can help absorb the expanding energies of the adolescent and direct these energies away from immature dependencies. A vocational commitment

---

[3]This alleged impact of jobs and responsibilities on adolescent idealism may underlie the popular phrase of the 1960s: "Never trust anyone over 30."

provides a focus for the young person's needs for fidelity, autonomy, initiative, and industriousness. However, making a vocational choice is not easy, and may indeed be one of the most disturbing aspects of adolescence (Erikson, 1968, p. 132). An initial response to this dilemma may be over-identification with the hero of a clique or crowd. Once individuals achieve an occupational identity, they are freed from overdependence on the peer group as well as the family.

These accomplishments take time. Erikson believes that, in order to achieve an integrated personality, adolescents need, above all else, a breathing period, a psychosocial moratorium. Erikson reminds his readers that, in spite of the apparent similarity between adolescent and neurotic "symptoms," adolescence is "not an affliction but a normative crisis" (1968, p. 163); the conflict characteristic of adolescence is also a sign of high potential for growth. Similarly, Piaget warns that we should not be disturbed by the extravagance and disequilibrium characteristic of adolescence. In fact, he holds that the passions and dreams of adolescence are the foundations of personal creativity (1968, p. 69).

Erikson and Piaget agree that there is a positive element in adolescent deviance, emotionality, and idealism. Piaget says, "In general, individuals who, between the ages of fifteen and seventeen, never constructed systems in which their life plans formed part of a vast dream of reform or who, at first contact with the material world, sacrificed their chimeric ideals to new adult interests, are not the most productive" (1968, p. 69). Erikson also believes that there is often an intrinsic relation between personal conflict and personal creativity. He holds, "For healthy individualism and devoted deviancy contain an indignation in the service of a wholeness that is to be restored, without which psychosocial evolution would be doomed" (1968, p. 248). He does not go so far as to say, as some psychologists have, that society is "sick," He does insist, however, that it is important to society that at least some of its members rebel against and refuse to accept some aspects of the "human condition."

Piaget and Erikson also agree that some environments are more conducive than others to the achievement of adolescent potential. In under-developed societies, individuals may never develop beyond the level of concrete operations (Piaget, 1972, p. 25). There is even some question as to whether members of all social classes within a developed society achieve formal operations. It seems likely, though, that "manual and technical workers" develop formal operational thinking on a vocational level that is different from, but equivalent to, the scientific and verbal level of better-educated adolescents (Piaget, 1972, p. 26). In order to test this assumption, formal tasks with a content familiar to these manual and technical workers will have to be developed.

Concerning emotional development, Erikson holds that identity "depends on the support which the young individual receives from the collective sense of identity characterizing the social groups significant to him: his class, his nation, his culture" (1968, p. 89). Thus, adolescence is probably least "stormy" for youth who are trained in roles and skills appropriate to our technological society (Erikson, 1968, p. 130). Conversely, adolescence may be most difficult for youngsters who feel deprived of opportunity by their environment. In fact, if society denies an adolescent the opportunity to develop a positive and self-respecting identity because of race or social class, the individual may be forced to adopt a negative identity that is based on all the roles that have been presented as most undesirable or dangerous and yet also as most inevitable for the individual (1968, p. 174). If society does not allow certain of its young people to experience a moratorium, they may create one for themselves by becoming members of a delinquent, but more accepting, subculture.

Thus, we come back to our emphasis on the interaction between individuals and their environments. In both Piaget's and Erikson's views, what individuals become depends not only on their human potential but also on the beneficence of their societies. The following chapters will consider what kinds of persons adolescents become as they develop as members of societies. Their potentials and achievements in the areas of cognition (Chapter Three), identity (Chapter Four), moral judgment and values (Chapter Five), and sexuality (Chapter Six), will be analyzed in light of current theory and research. The resulting picture of today's adolescent is based on a broad range of empirical studies as well as on the major theoretical viewpoints. The prevailing picture of adolescence, adolescent research, and adolescent theory all may change as the field of psychology develops.

Chapter Three

Logic and Cognition

Gradually, during adolescence, I developed a social conscience; I hated the oppression of blacks, felt guilt about being white, well fed and middle class, and was furious that my folks condoned the status quo by their inaction (although my inaction was just as bad as their brand of liberal lip service). I was strongly antimaterialistic, patching my jeans faithfully and asking my folks not to buy me birthday presents (although I drove the car with pleasure). My antimaterialistic motivation was probably due to purely personal motivations (feelings of guilt and inadequacy), as well as to more cognitive or "rational" ones and general unwitting adolescent conformity. I was quite idealistic—impatient with people who wouldn't withhold their taxes although they said they opposed the war, interested in the idea of communal living, disenchanted with "progress," and wishing to return to a relatively primitive lifestyle to restore meaning to life.

Qualitative changes in the structures of thinking may represent both the greatest achievement and the greatest burden of adolescence—and even of adulthood. It is the ability to think hypothetically, freed from immediate reality and detached from the concrete, that allows us to become scientists, philosophers, and poets. At the same time, it is the ability mentally to compare ourselves and our societies with other hypothetically possible selves and societies that allows us, even compels us, to become full-blown neurotics and avid social revolutionaries. The cognitive changes that can occur during adolescence are the basis for the ability to see not just how things are but also how they might, or should, be.

What is the nature of those cognitive achievements? The most complete and provocative answer to this question comes from Piaget, who argues that symbolic logic provides the tool for analyzing the structures inherent in all cognitive activity. Although Piaget's view is under attack by both logicians and psychologists, it is unquestionably the major impetus to theory and research in the area of adolescent and adult cognition. Consequently, we would like to present Piaget's theory of *formal operations* in enough detail to make its principal assumptions as clear and comprehensible as possible. We also will review briefly the chief criticisms of formal operational theory before considering adolescent thinking in broader terms.

Basic Concepts: Into Piagetian Territory

The description of adolescent logic in Chapter Two of this book does not begin to convey the complexity of the Piagetian view. Unsuspecting readers first examining Piaget's account of adolescent cognition (Inhelder & Piaget, 1958) might think themselves in a very strange land indeed. The language might seem more mathematical than verbal and the content more logical than psychological. Remember that Piaget began his investigations into cognition from a philosophical and biological base. He is not interested in what makes Carol smarter than Sue. Nor is it his goal to predict success in school from a score on a test. Instead, his is the approach of a genetic epistemologist; he has tried to discover and describe the basic structure of mental activity. His goal has been to answer the kinds of epistemological questions that intrigue philosophers—such as, what is the nature of mental life?

The tasks that Piaget has used to assess the highest level of human cognitive development (Inhelder & Piaget, 1958) are primarily scientific and mathematical. Subjects are presented with such esoteric-sounding problems as the equality of angles of incidence and reflection (that's a billiard game), the law of floating bodies (if you make a piece of clay small enough, will it float?), and the oscillation of a pendulum. To illustrate some Piagetian concepts, we'll describe the pendulum task in some detail.

In the pendulum problem, subjects are given a series of weights, strings of varying lengths, and a rod from which to suspend the weights. The subject's task is to discover the principle that determines how fast the weights swing back and forth or, more precisely, what determines how many times a weight can go back and forth within a given time period. In addition to length of string and weight, such variables as height of release point and force of push frequently are considered, especially by early adolescents or younger subjects.

In order to solve such a problem in a formal operational way, as opposed to a haphazard, trial-and-error, unreliable way, subjects must go through a series of trials in which they hold all but one of the possible variables constant. For example, the individual may vary the length of the string while keeping weight, height of release point, and force of push the same. Through a gradual process of exclusion, the individual eliminates those variables that are not causal in frequency of oscillation. Piaget calls this process *combinatorial thinking*—that is, thinking in terms of "all other things being equal" and arriving at proof of a principle by examining all possible combinations of variables.

Two sample protocols should help make the experimental situation more concrete. The first protocol is summarized in Table 1, complete with the subject's actions and verbalizations and our own "editorial" comments.

What would Piaget say about David's performance? First of all, David is not performing beyond a *concrete-operational* level. He is able to use the concrete operation of *seriation;* that is, he is able to compare the effects of different lengths or of different weights. However, he does not use the formal operation of *exclusion;* he is not able to separate the effects of length from the apparent effects of weight. He fails to vary the length of the string systematically while holding weight constant. Consequently, he fails to exclude or minimize weight as a determining variable. He is unable even to separate his own activity (strength of push) from the activity of the pendulum—a frequent error at the *preoperational* level.

Now let's consider a higher-level approach to the problem. Joshua starts out, as David did, with two weights of the same size, one on a short and one on a long string. He notes that the weight on the short string is swinging faster: "It's either the length of the string or the size of the weight that does it." He takes two different weights and first compares both on short strings and then both on long strings. He finally takes just one weight, raising it and lowering it on a single string. "Regardless of the size of the weight, it goes faster when the string is shorter." He concludes "It's the length, not the weight, that's important."

Joshua, unlike David, is functioning at a *formal-operational* level. He is able to vary one factor (length of string) while holding all others (weight, push) constant. He is thus able to exclude those factors that do not play a determining role in speed of oscillation. During this problem-solving process, Joshua makes several statements that Piaget would translate directly into the language of logic. His hypothesis that "It's either the length of the string or the size of the weight" expresses verbally the operation of *disjunction:* it is *a* or *b* or both. The logical operation of *implication* is illustrated by the statement "It goes faster when the string is shorter." "Regardless of the size of the weight" involves the operation of *independence* of one variable from another; *a* has an effect even if *b* does not.

These examples should suffice to provide the flavor of a Piagetian analysis. Piaget holds that the adolescent develops, in all, a total of 16 *binary propositional* operations. These operations are called propositional because

Table 1. Sample protocol for solution of the pendulum problem: David

Subject's Actions	Subject's Verbalizations	Comments
1. David takes two weights equal in heaviness; puts one on short and one on long string.	1. "This one (on the short string) should go faster because it covers a shorter distance."	1. Good start—only length of string is varied.
2. David next compares a heavy and a light weight, both on medium-length strings.	2. "I think, if I did it right, the heavier weight would oscillate slower than the lighter one. The heavier weight swings longer because it has more force but the distance it covers is the same."	2. Both weight and string lengths have been changed in relation to Step 1.
3. David puts four weights differing in heaviness on medium-length strings.	3. "I can't tell if the frequency of oscillation is affected by weight. The small one slows down faster than the larger ones."	3. Holding length of string constant while varying heaviness of weight should help him see that weight is not important; but a preconviction about the role of weight seems to inhibit this inference.
4. David compares a light weight on a short string with a heavy weight on a long string.	4. "I think the smaller weight oscillates faster in spite of the difference in the length of the string. The heavier the weight is, the faster it oscillates, and the shorter the string is, the faster it oscillates. Obviously, how hard I hit it makes a difference in oscillation, but I'm not sure how to measure that."	4. Making simultaneous changes in weight and length of string confounds the effects of the two variables and confuses David.

they center on propositions or hypotheses rather than concrete facts. They represent a higher level of abstraction than the concrete operations involved in classification and seriation that deal with directly observable properties of objects. The operations are called binary because they involve a relationship between two propositions. In our examples, the relationship is between the varying of weight and the speed of oscillation of a pendulum. Much of our everyday thinking is concrete and does not require these formal operations that, consequently, are frequently inactive. They represent potentials that can be called into play when individuals, because of their own level of development and because of the particular demands of a problem, find concrete solutions inadequate.

Formal operations are powerful problem-solving tools because of their unique structure. Piaget calls this structure *INRC:* identity, negation, reciprocity, and correlation. For example, in determining the weight of an object, for every operation (adding weight to the right side of a balance), there is an inverse or negating operation (taking that extra weight away again), a reciprocal operation (moving the weight in the left side of the balance farther from the fulcrum), and a correlative operation (moving the weight on the left side of the balance closer to the fulcrum). These physical "operations" of the subject become likely only when neurological operations have evolved to provide a conceptual basis for them.

What is most radical about Piaget's system is his conviction that he really is describing structures of the mind—not innate structures but structures that are elaborated as a result of the individual's interactions within an advanced society. It is not that the subject uses symbolic logic to solve problems. On the contrary, most subjects are unaware that their problem-solving behavior can be described in the language of propositional logic. Rather, the logician can describe behavior in the language of propositional logic for the very reason that the behavior reflects the underlying logic of the mind. The tools of symbolic logic simply allow the logician to describe in abstract, precise, and explicit terms what has been going on implicitly and unconsciously. Piaget (1972) has pointed out that, historically, mathematicians reasoned according to principles of which they were not consciously aware. For example, the INRC structure that Piaget attributes to adult thinking was implicit in Euclid's *Elements,* but it was not until the 19th century that Galois elaborated the conceptual tools—the concept of the INRC's structure—that allowed us to describe that structure. Just as the structure of a mathematical group allows us to describe and gain greater insight into the structure of propositional logic, the structure of a mathematical group allows us to describe and gain greater insight into the structure of man's mind. Formal thinking is, Piaget says, a "propositional calculus" (Inhelder & Piaget, 1958, p. 305).

Piaget argues that cybernetics, the science of computers, shows that the kind of structure he attributes to mental activity is truly a possibility. Computers have been designed by humans to perform combinatorial analyses and to operate according to principles of reversibility and reciprocity. Human scientists and logicians build computers according to principles that human scientists and logicians have discovered through the use of their minds and their brains. Piaget (1958) believes that cognitive structures are probably isomorphic (of the same structure) with neurological structures in the brain and with the mechanical structures of computers, which are designed in imitation of the brain.

The Logician's Critique

Regardless of Piaget's rationale for using symbolic logic to describe human thought, the reader may wonder whether a special language really is necessary to an understanding of problem solving. The question is an open one. Some logicians have been very critical of this aspect of Piaget's theory. It is not necessarily true that, if a logician is critical of Piaget's use of logic, then Piaget's use of logic is bad, inappropriate, or misleading. The logicians may be missing Piaget's point. Nevertheless, it may be worthwhile to consider the major criticism that logicians have offered.

There have been protests against "mistakes" (Ennis, 1975) and "ambiguity and obscurity" (Parsons, 1960) in Piaget's use of the language of formal logic. Sometimes Piaget uses the symbols p and q to refer to alternative independent (causal) variables. To use the example cited earlier, p may represent length of string and q may represent weight. The dependent variable, or outcome, is represented in this situation by x. Frequently, however, Piaget uses the same notation to refer to the relationship between an independent and dependent variable, which is quite different from the relationship between two independent variables. In this case, p may represent length of string and q frequency of oscillation, while x is not needed at all. In other words, in the first case, p and q refer to alternative independent hypotheses; in the second case, p and q refer to a single hypothetical causal relationship.

Piaget also has been criticized for assuming isomorphism (sameness of structure) among mathematical, logical, physical, neurological, and mental structures. Parsons (1960) holds that the connection between logic as built into the physical structure of a problem and logic as built into the cognitive structure of the problem solver is unclear and tenuous at best. Lunzer (1960) argues that, although certain relations may be fundamental to the logical analysis of a problem, there is no reason to assume that those same relations underlie the psychological evolution of understanding of the problem. It is his

conviction that the psychological properties involved in the child's elaboration of concepts must be examined separately from the logical properties
of the concepts.

Parsons (1960) also asks how far the isomorphism between problem
and problem solver is to be extended. If an individual solves problems that are
even more complicated than those considered by Piaget, then is a more
complicated algebra needed to characterize thought processes? Inhelder and
Piaget (1958) have spoken of "ternary" propositions and have considered
whether additional operations may be needed to describe formal thought
(p. 305), but they conclude that the language of propositional logic is sufficient. Arlin (1975) has argued that changes in thought structures continue
beyond the level of formal operations. Describing Piaget's formal operations
as a *problem-solving* stage, Arlin goes on to present evidence for the achievement of a *problem-finding* stage in some college seniors. However, the notion
that this achievement requires new cognitive structures probably represents a
misunderstanding of Piaget's structural concepts.

Finally, Parsons raises questions about problems that are not mathematical or scientific. Piaget has assumed that the formal operations utilized
in scientific problem solving are somehow involved in the more general
thinking of adolescents as they think about themselves, their society, and their
ideals. However, Piaget has not explained the details or mechanism of this
relationship. Wason and Johnson-Laird (1972) argue that Piaget does not pay
enough attention to the content, especially to the semantic content, of
problems and to the impact that content has on logical performance. Blasi and
Hoeffel (1974) strongly criticize Piaget's extension of the formal operational
model to adolescent personality. They note that the understanding of "the
purely possible" that typifies adolescent thinking is related to personal,
social, and civic life in ways that simply do not reflect the perfectly compen-
sated INRC system. Similarly, they argue that the "reflectivity" that adolescents show when solving formal operational problems seems very different in
nature from the "reflectivity" adolescents show when thinking about themselves. Their argument provides a conceptual underpinning for Peel's (1971)
finding that adolescent boys and girls consistently solve social problems at a
higher level of thinking than they use to solve physical problems.

Another major attack on Piaget's theory, from a logician's point of
view, focuses on the 16 binary operations. Here, two questions are asked
(Bynum, Thomas, & Weitz, 1972): (1) Do Inhelder and Piaget offer any
evidence that fully developed formal operational thinkers use all 16 binary
operations in solving problems? (2) Is there any reason to assume that fully
developed formal operational thinkers ever use all 16 binary operations?
Answers to these questions have been approached by both logical and
empirical means.

In one study, Weitz, Bynum, and Thomas (in press) attempted to determine empirically whether any of their subjects (aged 9, 12, and 16 years) would use all 16 postulated operations to solve the problem of invisible magnetism. The hypothesis that older subjects use more operations than younger subjects was also examined. The findings were interpreted as showing that all three age groups used the same five operations: conjunction (both p and q have an effect), disjunction (p or q or both have an effect), implication (if x happens, then p must have an effect), converse implication (it's p, if x happens), and independence (p has an effect regardless of whether or not q does). Of these, only two operations, conjunction and implication, were used with any regularity.

Weitz and associates reported that the number of operations subjects used did not differentiate the more developed from the less developed problem solvers. However, these age groups did differ in the complexity and integration of the operations used. Unfortunately, no examples were provided to illustrate different levels of complexity and integration. Weitz and associates concluded that there are identifiable developmental changes in reasoning. They rejected the notion that what evolves is the elaboration of 16 binary operations, holding instead that what changes is the quality and complexity of a few common operations. This conclusion seems to be not so much an empirically demonstrated finding as a decision made about how much inference about operations is desirable and helpful.

It should be apparent that at least some logicians have reservations concerning the formal aspects of Piaget's analysis. However, they generally would agree with the psychologists who hold that Piaget's theory would be equally important and not substantially different without the extensive use of the concepts and symbolism of logic (Lefrancois, 1972; Lovell, 1961). Like many psychologists, these logicians see great insights and useful constructs in Piaget's description of adolescent problem solving. In particular, there is considerable agreement that the adolescent develops the potential to reason with propositions and not just with facts, to solve problems by isolating variables, to look consciously for laws, to deal with abstractions such as proportions and correlations, and to think about thought itself. There is also agreement that adolescents use their cognitive processes—whatever form they may take—to think about themselves, their relationships, their futures, and their worlds. These broader changes are illustrated in an autobiographical statement.

> Starting in early adolescence, I did an enormous amount of reading that seriously affected my ideas, thoughts, and opinions but only gradually affected my behavior. I was stuck in the role of a good, studious girl and I knew it. Eventually, I opened my eyes and let my feelings out. I protested against the war. I stopped going to Catholic church, but I joined a discussion group in the Unitarian church for a while. I voiced hostility

toward the hypocrisy that I saw in my teachers and my parents. This may
have been a change in my intellectual development because I questioned
everything and found that more and more was phony.

Let's consider what is known about adolescent thought, both in the
more specific sense of formal operations and in the broader sense just
described. We will not attempt to resolve the ongoing controversy over
whether the development of formal operations underlies all other aspects of
adolescent cognition. Nor will we assume that adolescent performance on
non-Piagetian tasks tells us anything about the development of formal
operations. We simply will summarize the current picture of adolescent
thinking and the factors affecting it.

Cognitive Development during the Adolescent Years

Piaget believes that an integrated and coordinated system of formal
operations, that has its foundations in infancy, evolves slowly during adolescence. If he is correct, one would expect more older than younger adolescents
to solve the pendulum problem, and similar tasks, in a formal operational
way. And, indeed, more 14-year-olds than 13-year-olds (Tisher, 1971) and
more 17-year-olds than 14-year-olds (Dulit, 1972) can solve Piagetian
problems in a formal manner. As already noted, there is some evidence that
this improvement in problem solving is not a function of an increase in the
number of operations used but rather of an increase in the flexibility and
coordination of just a few "common" operations (Weitz, Bynum, Thomas, &
Steger, in press).

During the junior high and high school years, adolescents improve
their ability to perform in a wide variety of intellectual tasks. They become
more flexible in their thinking; they are better able, for example, to classify
the same objects in many different ways (Elkind, Barocas, & Johnsen, 1969)
and to shift from one kind of classification to another (Elkind, 1966). They
also become more adept at concept-attainment tasks—that is, intellectual
puzzles that require determining which of a series of concepts is "correct"
(Yudin & Kates, 1963)—and at transitivity problems, such as: If A is bigger
than B and B is smaller than C, which is biggest and which is smallest? (Glick
& Wapner, 1968). They come to do better on all forms of Piaget's conservation problems, recognizing that mass, weight, and volume remain the same
despite changes in shape (Elkind, 1961).

The development of formal operations is generally not complete by
the end of high school. Even among college students there appear to be many
individuals who cannot solve some problems in a fully formal way (Elkind,

1962). At the same time, there is some evidence that college-age adolescents and young adults can solve Piaget's conservation problems better than older adults (Kuhn, Langer, Kohlberg, & Haan, 1971; Papalia, 1972) and that some older adults are not able to solve Piaget's formal problems at all (Dulit, 1972; Graves, 1972).

It should be apparent that a reliable prediction cannot be made from chronological age as to the achievement of a developmental task or function. What kinds of things determine why one 14-year-old can solve a problem in a formal operational way while another cannot? In the example of the pendulum problem cited earlier in this chapter, why did one college freshman, Joshua, exhibit formal operations while another college freshman, David, did not? We will discuss some of the variables that seem to make a difference, such as IQ and sex, as well as the limits in usefulness of these variables.

IQ and MA

Two variables that seem to be associated with when, and if, one achieves formal operations are the intelligence quotient and the related variable of mental age. Although there are vast differences both in underlying assumptions and in measurement techniques between the Piagetian and psychometric, or IQ testing, approach to intelligence, there frequently seem to be relationships between the two kinds of measures. There are several good discussions of the differences between Piagetian and psychometric types of assessment—for example, those of Furth (1970) and Voyat (1969). Briefly, the main position is that IQ tests measure the *products* of learning and not, as commonly thought, the *potential* for learning. Piagetian tasks are concerned with the processes of problem solving. The concern in IQ testing is with right or wrong answers. The concern in Piagetian testing is with how children reason and why they make whatever judgments they make.

Many studies that employ both Piagetian and psychometric techniques find that the relationship between them is statistically significant, but what this relationship means remains to be explained. For example, retarded children and adolescents, with IQs of from 50 to 75, show delayed development in their performance on a variety of Piagetian tasks and are unable to achieve formal operations at all (Jackson, 1965; Stephens, 1972). Similarly, adolescents of normal intelligence are not as successful on Piagetian tasks as are their gifted peers (Dulit, 1972). In general, studies seem to indicate that the attainment of formal operations is related more closely to mental age than to chronological age (Jackson, 1965).

Some investigators report a statistically significant relationship between success on Piagetian tasks and IQ (Elkind, 1961; Goodnow, 1962).

Others report that the increasing efficiency of youth on concept-formation tasks is more closely related to MA than to IQ (Neimark, 1970; Neimark & Lewis, 1968). There is also evidence that, even with MA held constant or with CA (chronological age) held constant, adolescents of normal intelligence do better on a variety of reasoning tasks than adolescents who are retarded (Stephens, 1972) or who have difficulty with reading (Elkind, Barocas, & Rosenthal, 1968).

In sum, whatever it is that IQ tests measure—and that is the subject of considerable controversy—individuals who do better on IQ tests also seem to be successful on Piagetian tasks at younger ages than peers with lower IQs. Evidence that Piagetian and psychometric tests simply are not measuring the same thing—"intelligence"—comes from factor-analytic studies indicating that the two represent separate and distinct underlying factors (Stephens, McLaughlin, Miller, & Glass, 1972). Thus, the exact nature of the relationship between the two approaches to intelligence remains to be resolved. One could argue that the same children who have experiences that help them do well on tests, including IQ tests, have experiences that facilitate the development of formal operations.

One senses a particular kind of educational background and advantage in the following young woman's comments. One suspects that she would show average or above average performance both on IQ tests and on other cognitive tasks.

> I learned many new things and felt strongly about some of them, although I simultaneously felt that I really *didn't* have answers and so any belief or opinion was open to discussion and change. My mind was active, probing the usual philosophical questions and my feelings about myself and/or other people. Happiness came in the forms of personal creativity (writing or playing music I liked) and of rare communion gained with other people in long talks. I got angry at people whose lives or actions denied things or people about which I felt strongly. I hated the war supporters, suburbanites, blatant bigots, consumers, anti-intellectuals. . . .

Sex Differences

The role of gender in the development of formal operations also poses a puzzle. The available data are simply inconsistent. Some studies find that boys are superior to girls in the development of formal operations (Dulit, 1972; Field & Cropley, 1969). Others report no sex differences whatsoever, sometimes on the very same tasks used in the studies reporting sex differences (Brainerd, 1971; Jackson, 1965; Kuhn, Langer, Kohlberg, & Haan, 1971; Tisher, 1971). Some studies provide elaborate explanations for the occurrence of sex differences in adolescent cognitive development (Elkind, 1961, 1962).

Others do not even bother to evaluate sex differences. Moreover, there is evidence that the performance of subjects of either sex can be affected by the sex of the examiner (White & Mervis, 1975).

No one any longer suggests that those sex differences that do occur reflect innate discrepancies in intellectual potential. Instead, psychological, or motivational, explanations are proposed to account for such findings. Elkind's view is that success on intellectual tasks generally is considered inappropriate to the female sex role. Consequently, young females concerned with becoming women do not perform well (Elkind, 1961). (How many of our women readers once were warned by their mothers not to be too smart or they would scare the boys away?) Elkind (1962) reports that the proportion of females doing well on Piagetian tasks increases over the college years and argues that those females who remain in college adopt nontraditional roles. While this assertion may sound convincing, Elkind's procedures and findings have been attacked strongly in a study that found no such sex differences (White & Friedman, 1976).

While the sex differences reported by Elkind may not be reliable, it nevertheless is likely that cognitive performances can be affected by motivational influences. Some college women do seem to do better when problems involve "feminine" rather than "masculine" content—for instance, yards of material to cut rather than miles to go before you sleep (Milton, 1959). Others do better if the problem is presented by a female rather than a male experimenter or if a male experimenter gives them a "pep talk" (Hoffman & Maier, 1966). While some high school boys do better than their female peers on the problem of conservation of volume, the girls may show more abstract thinking when the problem pertains to a real-life interpersonal situation (Higgens-Trenk & Gaite, 1971). There is also extensive evidence that, prior to adolescence, girls do better than boys on several intellectual tasks and in school.

It is difficult to say anything final about how sex differences influence the achievement of formal operations. Where such differences exist, they may be linked to rather long-term socialization influences on motivation or to more short-term motivational influences, including the attitude and behavior of the experimenter. Certainly evidence from a variety of sources (Klineberg, 1967; Lessing, 1972) suggests that motivational factors can interact with both age and sex in influencing adolescent cognitive judgments.

The Nature of the Task

One hazard facing everyone who attempts to interpret findings of differences among groups in the attainment of formal operations is an underestimation of the role of task variables. It is dangerous to infer from differences in performance on a given set of tasks that more boys than girls employ formal operations. It is just as dangerous to assume that more Swiss adolescents use formal operations than their counterparts in North America (Dulit, 1972), England (Jackson, 1965; Lovell, 1961), or Australia (Tisher, 1971). There is ample evidence that the number of subjects in any group who display formal thinking is very much dependent on the particular task used to measure it. Some problems are rather consistently more difficult than others. No valid conclusions about differences among groups in formal-operational ability can be reached until more is known about formal-operational performance as a function of task content.

Unfortunately, it is impossible to rank order all tests of formal operations for level of difficulty. Different investigators have selected or developed different tasks as indices of formal operations, have presented them in different forms, and have administered them in different ways. Out of the whole mishmash of evidence, it is difficult to say more than that adolescents find it easier to solve verbal and mathematical analogies than to solve the pendulum problem (Lunzer, 1965) and find it easier to solve the pendulum problem than to perform several other of the Piagetian tasks (Kuhn, Langer, Kohlberg, & Haan, 1971). Nevertheless, as long as investigators continue to report that their subjects show formal operations on some tasks but not on others, one should beware of easy judgments as to who "has" formal operations and who does not.

Training in Formal Operational Thinking

Formal operations, according to Piaget, evolve "naturally" during adolescence, given appropriate environmental stimulation and interaction. Does that mean it is impossible to teach preadolescents solutions to formal-operational problems? Perhaps not. If preadolescents are at an age when the transition to formal operations may have already begun (10 to 11 years) and if they are taught helpful rules or trained in the solution of sample problems, then many of them do seem capable of learning to "act like scientists"—to solve problems in a formal-operational way (Siegler, Liebert, & Liebert, 1973). On the other hand, there is evidence (Tomlinson-Keasey, 1972) that, even though 11-year-old girls can be trained to solve some problems in a formal-operational way, these gains are soon lost. Older women seem able to show short-term gains in level of thinking as a result of training, but these gains are also lost. Only in college women does training in formal-operational thinking seem to lead to relatively stable changes in mode of thought. Comparable research with males has not been done yet. Inferring changes in cognitive *structures* as a result of training, then, seems at best a risky conclusion. Undoubtedly, there are experiences that facilitate the development of formal operations and of cognitive achievements in general, but the nature of productive training experiences remains very much open to question.

Other Cognitive Achievements and Disruptions

Piaget has emphasized the more scientific and mathematical aspects of adolescent thinking. Other researchers have attempted to analyze more everyday expressions of the ability to deal with abstractions, to isolate and compare interrelated aspects of a situation, to think of several factors in combination with one another, and to deduce possibilities from a purely hypothetical premise. For example, Shaffer (1930) examined age trends in the ability to interpret cartoons abstractly and correctly. Goldman (1965) conducted a similar analysis of the ability to interpret religious stories, while Freides, Fredenthal, Grisell, and Cohen (1963) looked at the development of proverb interpretation.

Age changes in interpersonal evaluations also have been studied. With development, young people get better at speculating about motives underlying behavior (Gollin, 1958), making mature judgments about the kindness of any given behavior (Baldwin & Baldwin, 1970), and predicting what their friends might say about them in any given situation (deJung & Meyer, 1963).

The increasing ability of adolescents to differentiate between the kind of person they see themselves as really being and the kind of person they would like to be (Katz & Zigler, 1967; Piers & Harris, 1964) may be related to the tendency of some adolescents to show signs of schizophrenia. Lidz (1974) says:

> Feeling hopeless about the future and permeated by despair of ever becoming a person in his own right, or terrified at responsibilities he cannot assume, the youth develops more elaborate fantasy solutions and regresses cognitively as well as emotionally. Poorly grounded in reality testing and with tenuous boundaries between the self and others, he finds a way out of his real developmental dilemma by falling back to childhood forms of egocentric cognition [p. 97].

Adolescents diagnosed as mentally ill are characterized by such a severe disruption in cognitive functioning that the individual may seem to be operating on a preoperational level (Feffer, 1959; Lerner, Bie, & Lehrer,

1972). Suicidal adolescents seem more impaired than nonsuicidal adolescent patients on some problem-solving tasks (Levenson & Neuringer, 1971).

Most adolescents do not become suicidal or mentally ill. Many, however, develop defense mechanisms not available to the younger child. For example, they may rely excessively on intellectualization—an extreme emphasis on objective judgment and technical knowledge (Freud, 1966). The relationship between cognitive development and emotional-defensive development can be seen in the comments of this college woman:

> It seems that any new thing I picked up took the form of an obsession that I could not shrug off, even when I wanted to. My obsessional nature even generalized to religion, where I was a Jewish fanatic. My friends, who for the most part were Reform Jews, knew better than to discuss Judaism with me. In high school, I told my biology teacher at the beginning of the term that I refused to study evolution. It took much persuasion to convince me that I should learn more in depth about what I was disagreeing with. I had a very great sense of what I thought was right and became quite upset and confused if I was proven wrong. My personality was characterized by self-righteousness, strivings for perfection, obsessions, compulsions, and emotionality.

In this chapter, we have emphasized qualitative changes in cognitive functioning. As illustrated by several of the autobiographical statements, some adolescents are intensely aware of changes in their own modes of thinking. The statements also demonstrate that some adolescents are intensely aware of themselves in general; they are self-exploring, sometimes self-critical, and sometimes self-accepting. The self, in later stages of adolescent development, holds an important place in the content of adolescent thought. We think that cognitive changes, physical changes, and changes in social pressures and interactions all converge to make identity a focal point for most adolescents. It is this topic that we will explore next.

Chapter Four

Change and Identity

I spent early adolescence wondering why I didn't have the adjust-ment, rebellion, and generation-gap problems that others frequently com-plained about. And I spent middle adolescence wishing I didn't have them. My middle adolescence seemed polarized—great sadness and anger and great joy and happiness. I felt in extremes.

The transition from middle to late adolescence seems clearly marked—moving to college, leaving parents and friends, dealing with the changes of being on my own. Late adolescence was intense but not nearly as stormy. Conflicts centered around separating from my parents, choosing a career, and deciding whether to marry the person I loved. It was a time of introspection but also of forming my own life-style. Making decisions was hard, but I was making them, and that made a difference.

The term *identity* has become a part of the popular language of our culture. Who am I? Where am I going? When will I find myself? How will I get my head together? These are the kinds of questions that are associated with the adolescent *identity crisis*. Yet Erikson, who coined the term *identity crisis*, holds that the kind of extreme *identity consciousness* implied in the questions above is the exception rather than the rule in adolescence. Con-sequently, it seems imperative to clarify the meaning of identity and identity crisis in Erikson's formulations. Also important is an understanding of the biological events that provide an impetus to the identity issue. In addition, we will discuss the major findings about the ways in which adolescents respond to identity formation. Finally, we will consider professional and occupational choices as a form of resolution to the identity crisis.

There are four elements in Erikson's use of the term *identity* that we want to emphasize. (1) Identity is not static; it is a truly developmental process. However, the core of identity formation during adolescence is continuity between past and future. (2) Identity is as much an attribute of society as of the individual. Adolescent identity crises revolve around the acceptance by society and by the individual of the individual's choice of a place within society. (3) For the most part, individuals are not conscious of their own identity development. (4) The criterion for successful resolution of the identity crisis is the achievement of an ethical capacity that allows the individual to take responsibility for the next generation. We will elaborate briefly on each of these points.

Identity is not something a person just *has*. Consequently, it is different from the more static, although related, terms of *self-concept, self-esteem,* or *role* (Erikson, 1968). Identity formation is an organic process; that is, it evolves and changes over time. It has its roots in the baby's identification of self with mother, but it must develop to the point where the growing person can let go of parents and become an individual in his or her own right. This increasing independence of young people from their families is facilitated by identification with their age-mates; but identity goes beyond these identifications also.

Identity formation, because it is a developmental process, involves different issues at different life stages. The particular crisis of adolescence centers on continuity in a context of change—continuity between what the changing individual was and will be. During puberty, adolescents are well on their way to physical adulthood. They quickly gain the capacity for full sexual relations and for reproduction, and these biological changes are accompanied by a change in social expectations and roles. In some societies, the new biological and social status of the individual is confirmed in a clear and straightforward fashion in puberty rites. In these instances, some apprenticeship into adult responsibilities may still be necessary, but there is usually little question as to where the maturing youngster fits within the fabric of society. Identity is achieved rather easily, and the transition between childhood and adulthood may be relatively brief. It also is less likely to be a time of turmoil.

However, as Erikson (1968) points out, it is impossible to separate personal growth from communal change or adolescent crises from more general social crises, as individual and group identities help define each other. Rapid technological change modifies social roles faster than youth can move into, or rebel against, them (Erikson, 1968). Such social change must be accompanied by stress to the individuals who are involved in identity formation, and, in turn, the years following puberty are likely to be a true adolescent period marked by frustration and stress in individual identity development.

Not all of the social or personal stress that is a part of developing societies is experienced by adolescents as a "who am I?" phenomenon. Much of the work of the ego—integrating different selves, roles, and relation-ships—goes on outside the conscious awareness of the individual. Indeed, the extreme identity consciousness of some young people in North American society today may be as much the result of the unsettled nature of our society's goals and purposes and the focus of the media on youth as it is an outcome of a developmental stage. In many cases, this identity consciousness may reflect society's failure to confirm its adolescents in productive roles; in other cases, it may reflect other psychological and social problems faced by adolescents.

If identity is a problem, it is also society's problem: youth become the society of the future, responsible for succeeding generations. The identities formed by young people maintain some of the characteristics of a broader communal identity. In "primitive" societies, the inventory of identities is static and limited (Erikson, 1968) but adapted to the needs of those societies—at least as long as they are protected from the encroachments of "civilization." Even in modern society alternatives tend to be limited. Erikson worries about the future when he sees the kinds of technocrat-bureaucrat identities that are adopted by many young people today.

Individual identity, then, reflects the interaction of biological, social, and ego processes (Erikson, 1968). The biological changes of puberty signify both to the individual ego and to the larger society that young people are no longer identical to what they were before. That is, with puberty, individuals are no longer children, and both they and the people around them must deal with the significant physical changes taking place. We would like to describe some of these fundamental biological changes before we go on to describe individual resolutions to the identity crises engendered by puberty.

Physical Changes

The beginning of adolescence is usually linked to puberty, but puberty itself is a complex and variable set of processes. Even the definition of puberty varies considerably. At the core of most definitions is reference to the maturation of the reproductive system. Also frequently included in a definition of puberty is the achievement of general physical maturity.

The word *puberty* comes from the Latin word *pubis,* which refers either to the lower abdomen or to hair on the groin. *Pubescence* comes from the Latin word *pubescens,* which means becoming hairy or downy (McCand-less, 1970). However, some important physical changes associated with puberty typically begin before the growing girl or boy becomes "downy." Moreover, while many people think *menarche,* or first menstruation, in the girl and ejaculation in the boy are the first signs of puberty, there are, in fact, much earlier signs.

In most boys, the first indication of puberty, usually starting around the age of 12 but sometimes beginning as early as 10 or as late as 13½ years, is enlargement of the testicles, accompanied by enlargement and reddening of the scrotum (Tanner, 1970). Growth of pubic hair—first downy, then pigmented, and then increasingly curly and profuse—follows fairly soon after the beginning of testicular enlargement (Schonfeld, 1971). The acceleration of penis growth begins later, at about 13 years. Maximum penis growth is generally achieved at 15 years, at which time the penis is likely to be slightly larger than it is during adulthood (Tanner, 1962). First ejaculation, either spontaneous or induced, occurs at an average age of just under 14 years (Schonfeld, 1971). Here, as on all indices, there is considerable variation. In one large sample of boys, first ejaculation was experienced as early as 11 and as late as 16 years (Kinsey, Pomeroy, & Martin, 1948). Facial hair and axillary hair begin to appear around the age of 14, followed by the gradual growth of the remainder of body hair. Voice change usually doesn't begin until 14½ or 15 years and takes several years for completion.

In most girls the first manifestation of puberty, corresponding to testicular development in boys but occurring much earlier, is enlargement of the ovaries (Schonfeld, 1971). Since the size of the ovaries is not easily observed, the arrival of puberty usually is linked to the appearance of the breast bud around the age of 11 (Tanner, 1970). Simultaneous with breast development, but often less noticeable to the girl as well as to others, are changes in the uterus and vagina. Like the boy's penis, the girl's labia and clitoris enlarge. Her genital growth usually is completed two years earlier than the boy's. The growth of pubic hair generally follows the beginnings of breast development. As is also true of boys, the growth of underarm hair follows the appearance of pubic hair, frequently by a year or more. Menarche comes relatively late in this sequence, at an average age of 12¾ years. Acne appears by late adolescence in about 80% of all boys and girls.

The *adolescent growth spurt,* a rapid increase in height and weight after a period of relatively slow development during middle childhood, begins before many of the pubertal changes just discussed—at about the age of 9 in girls, and 11 in boys. Because of their head start, most girls become heavier than their male peers by the age of 10 and taller by 11 (Tanner, 1970). It is not until the age of 14 that most boys become taller and heavier than their female counterparts. The adolescent growth spurt lasts for an average of two to four years, with some gradual growth thereafter. During the period of most rapid development, boys gain an average of about eight inches in height (Bernard, 1971).

Girls generally achieve their adult stature between the ages of 15 and 18 years, and boys between 17 and 20 years. Probably because of improved nutrition, adolescents today are taller and sexually more mature at a younger age than adolescents in past generations. The growth spurt begins earlier, the rate of growth is faster, and maximum growth is reached about two years sooner than it was two or three generations ago (Schonfeld, 1971). These changes in rate of maturation have been accompanied by an earlier interest in sex, earlier dating and courtship, earlier sexual intercourse, earlier marriage, and an increase in venereal disease and illegitimate births (Muus, 1970).

Physical differences among individuals become more noticeable after the adolescent growth spurt. Tall and short fourth-graders differ by only a few inches, but tall and short young men may differ by as much as a foot (Dwyer & Mayer, 1968–69). Physical differences between the sexes also become more dramatic. Before adolescence, boys and girls of the same body size and shape are about the same in strength; after adolescence, boys are much stronger (Tanner, 1971).

The adolescent growth spurt is not without its physical—as well as psychological—costs. The relatively rapid increase in height, weight, and muscle, and the onset of menstruation in the girl, add to the body's need for protein, calcium, iron, and other nutrients (Lambert et al., 1972). Much of the apathy, fatigue, and listlessness of some adolescents can be linked to the acceleration of physical growth, especially if their tremendous appetites do not lead them to fill up on adequately nutritious food.

Psychological Experience

Just as significant as these physical changes are the ways in which adolescents respond to and deal with their own development. We discussed in Chapter Three some of the cognitive developments that take place during adolescence. These cognitive developments may be critical in the adolescent's experience of change. Tanner (1971) states that the years from 12 to 16 are physically the most eventful ones in the lives of young people, arguing that "Admittedly during fetal life and the first year or two after birth development occurred still faster, and a sympathetic environment was probably even more crucial, but the subject himself was not the fascinated, charmed, or horrified spectator that watches the developments, or lack of developments, of adolescence" (p. 907). This self-consciousness about their changing bodies is probably an important part of adolescents' concerns about who they are becoming.

Bernard (1971) wonders where the "myth" and "misconception" of adolescent "awkwardness" come from. It seems quite possible that this "myth" comes from adolescents themselves, who may need time to get used to their somewhat abruptly changing bodies. A sense of awkwardness may stem particularly from the fact that the adolescent growth spurt is not a smooth and uniform process. Different parts of the body begin to develop at different times and then proceed to develop at different rates. First to reach adult size are the head, hands, and feet. Pubescent youngsters distressed by large hands and feet will not have to suffer too long before they, like puppies, grow into their extremities. Next, the legs lengthen and complete their spurt, followed by a widening of the hips, especially in girls. Later in the sequence, the shoulders broaden, especially in boys. Then trunk length and chest depth increase, so that shirts and jackets still are being outgrown when boys have stopped outgrowing the length of their pant legs, and girls are finding their dresses short waisted (Lambert et al., 1972; Tanner, 1971). Even the eyeballs of the adolescent develop unevenly, leading to a passing period of near-sightedness in many young people.

Some real psychological distress may be attached to the adolescent growth process because of the rather wide range of individual differences in the timing of pubertal changes. Among girls aged 11, 12, and 13 years, and among boys aged 13, 14, and 15 years, there is tremendous physical variability, ranging from fully preadolescent status to nearly complete physical maturity (Tanner, 1971). It even is possible to find perfectly healthy girls who have reached adult status in breast and pubic hair development, who are two years past their adolescent growth spurt, and who have not yet begun menstruating (Tanner, 1971). Such a delay must be of considerable worry to some.

In societies like ours, where status and privileges are accorded to those who are "grown-up," slow maturers may feel inadequate indeed. At the same time, there seem to be a number of advantages and disadvantages attached to both early and late maturation. A woman senior reminisces:

> Early adolescence was extremely difficult. I was very embarrassed about my changing body. I perspired profusely and was very embarrassed about it. I also felt very uncomfortable about menstrual hygiene at school; there was always the fear that the boys would know. All this discomfort came through in giggles, for I was incredibly silly!

During the high school years, early-maturing boys seem to have a number of advantages over late-maturing boys. In some schools, most of the student leaders are drawn from the group of early maturers. These boys are treated by adults and other children as if they were older and more responsible, and they gain status with relatively little effort (Jones & Bayley, 1950). Early maturers are more likely than late maturers to induce first ejaculation and begin almost immediately a pattern of regular sexual behavior

(McCandless, 1970). However, they have longer to wait from physical maturation to adult occupational and marital status, and there is some evidence for a tendency among early maturers to report less happiness in marriage (Ames, 1957, reported in McCandless, 1970).

Given the greater prestige frequently accorded early-maturing boys, it is not surprising that many late maturing boys have negative self-concepts and generally low self-esteem. They frequently feel inadequate, rejected, and dominated. Almost all of the girls and most of the boys of the same age mature before them and begin to gain social and emotional experience in heterosexual relationships before them (Dwyer & Mayer, 1968–69). As to their parents, late maturers may feel both prolonged dependency needs and a desire to rebel against any parental overprotectiveness (Mussen & Jones, 1957). Late maturers are viewed by others as being less physically attractive and more attention-seeking, restless, and bossy (Jones & Bayley, 1950). In an effort to compensate for their relatively less favorable status, they may behave in ways that serve only to solidify that status. These relationships among physical maturation, social status, and personality seem closely tied to a North American cultural emphasis on competence, achievement, and compe-tition—all of which are related to physical size and strength. The effects of early and late maturing are much stronger among North American than among Italian boys (Mussen & Boutourline-Young, 1964).

Moreover, how individuals feel about their physical development probably depends in part on the subculture of their school. In many schools, success in sports is far more important than success in academics (clearly *not* tied to physique), reflecting the anti-intellectualism rampant in some segments of society. In some schools, the boy who is considered to be the best scholar does not want to think of himself as a brilliant student nearly so much as the best athlete wants to think of himself as an athletic star (Coleman, 1961, 1969). Female scholars seem to be even more reluctant to accept an image of themselves as brilliant students. After all, it is adolescent folk-knowledge that smart girls scare off boys. In schools that emphasize sports achievement, rate of maturation may play a much larger role in the development of self-concept than in other schools, where it's O.K. to be an "intellectual."

Early-maturing girls are faced with the problem that few of the other girls and almost none of the boys of their age are maturing at the same rate as they are (Dwyer & Mayer, 1968–69). These girls frequently date older boys and may find themselves in situations that they are not psychologically ready for. Treated by peers and adults as budding young women, early-maturing girls seem to develop a precocious sense of identity as prospective wives and mothers (Douvan & Adelson, 1966). Thus, girls who mature early may date younger and express an early commitment to a very traditional and stereotyped view of the female role in life. The goal of such girls is not to develop meaningful friendships with other girls, not to make plans for a career, not to think about who they are and where they are going, but rather to get married and have children (Douvan & Adelson, 1966).

Other studies (Jones & Mussen, 1958; Weatherly, 1964) have found that in girls there are fewer clear-cut differences between early and late maturers than in boys. Neither physical acceleration nor physical retardation seems consistently advantageous to social status in girls, particularly in the early adolescent years (Faust, 1960). In at least some cases, prepubertal girls are seen by their peers as being more popular, more friendly, and more assured than pubertal or postpubertal girls (Faust, 1960). Moreover, the tendency of early-maturing girls to "go to fat" (McCandless, 1970) must cause considerable discomfort for many of them.

It seems likely that boys respond differently than girls not only to early versus late maturation but also to the totality of physical changes that take place during adolescence. In the context of North American society, menstruation probably is linked to the issue of potential and future parenthood more vitally than is any comparable development in boys. In the boy, manifest visibility and palpability must make his genitals more overtly sexual than are any corresponding organs in the girl. Although the data are scanty, it seems clear, for example, that becoming pregnant has significantly different social and psychological consequences and meanings from impregnating. Both boys and girls must cope with radical physical changes, and both must anticipate becoming autonomous adults filling responsible social roles. However, differences in their biological makeup seem to be accompanied by differences in psychological experience as well as in social expectations.

How do adolescents feel about what is happening when everything, inside and out, is in flux? Radical changes are occurring in their bodies, their cognitive approach is shifting, and all social contacts seem to be changing. A number of reactions are possible, depending on the particular phase of adolescence that is being negotiated and the individual's previous psychosocial developmental history. Also important are the opportunities, demands, and sources of recognition available within society.

It is fairly widely accepted that in our society early adolescence, from the ages of 11 or 12 to 14 or 15 years, is likely to be experienced as difficult by many adolescents and their parents (Hamburg, 1974; Offer, 1969). Added to the stresses of puberty are the pressures of a new and different social institution—the junior high school. No longer can students spend their school days in the relative comfort of the self-contained classroom, guided—or ruled— by the consistent presence of a teacher who may have also represented to the child a mother or father figure. Achievement pressures increase, and the student must face six or seven different teachers, and six or seven different courses every day. Parents, like children themselves, see junior high school as a new world, symbolizing the end of childhood and the beginning of adolescence (Hamburg, 1974).

The stresses inherent in the overlapping discontinuities of early adolescence are reflected in a sudden drop in academic performance following entry into junior high school (Armstrong, 1964, cited in Hamburg, 1974; Finger & Silverman, 1966). Apparently aware of the hazards ahead of them, sixth-graders express a number of worries about the transition into junior high school. Hamburg lists these as: fear of academic failure; insecurity about dealing with a different teacher and different groups of students every hour; concern about being able to make and keep friends; ignorance about what will be expected of them now that they're becoming "teenagers"; and confusion about the bigness and complexity of the new school and its routines, including, in some cases, fears of actually becoming lost and failing to appear for classes.

The academic difficulties that many students experience in junior high school may stem partially from emotional concerns about their changing bodies and changing roles. Difficulties also may stem from inappropriate expectations on the part of the teachers—in particular, from too abrupt an introduction of abstract subject matter. Only beginning the transition to new forms of thinking, many junior high school students are uncertain and often unaware of their abilities to generalize, to use symbols, and even to role-play abstract situations (Hamburg, 1974). Teachers often complain about the difficulty of teaching the boisterous, obstreperous, often uninhibited junior high school students, without recognizing that they may be contributing to the difficulties of this transitional age. Parents, ambivalent about the changing status of their growing youngsters or too anxious to promote the independence of their fledglings, may fail to provide adequate emotional support. In addition, peers who gain a new role as confidants and models for identification are themselves too immature and rigid to guide each other through the stresses of the pubertal years.

During middle adolescence, or, roughly, the high school years, cognitive development may catch up with academic demands, allowing the young person to deal better with abstract subject matter. Although for many "average" and "healthy" young men there may be disagreements with parents over hair length, clothing styles, dating hours, and use of the family car, there is no major "generation gap" over significant political and moral issues (Offer, 1969). For such male adolescents, growth through the high school years, and beyond, is relatively continuous and characterized by close family ties (Offer & Offer, 1975). Unfortunately, while Offer (1969) and Offer and Offer (1975) have provided a rather full picture of the ways that boys negotiate adolescence and late adolescence, there are no comparable data for females.

While adolescence is smooth for many young men, for others development is less continuous, and social relationships, academic concerns, and other involvements are characterized by abrupt and intense changes that rise in peaks and decline rapidly (Offer & Offer, 1975). Adolescent males in this group are more emotional, more prone to depression, more likely to experience intermittent periods of turmoil, and more variable in their sense of self-esteem than males in the "continuous growth" group described above. They also are more likely to have disagreements with parents over basic issues such as religion or academic success. Such young men express real fears of their emerging sexual impulses and delay entry into intimate physical relationships.

Finally, there are adolescent males who seem completely normal and healthy at the age of 14 but whose development over the next few years can be best described as "tumultuous" (Offer & Offer, 1975). These youths clearly fit into the pattern of identity diffusion described by Erikson. They are subject to recurrent self-doubts and escalating conflicts with their parents and are inconsistent both in academic performance and in interpersonal relationships. They are moody, mistrustful of the adult world, anxious, and dependent on their peer group for emotional support. While they frequently begin dating early, they often use their girl friends as "mother figures" and fail to develop balanced relationships. At the same time, many such youths are highly sensitive and introspective and just as "well-adjusted" in terms of overall functioning as youths who experience adolescence more smoothly.

Late adolescence, beginning roughly with the end of high school, is the phase of adolescence during which an *overt* identity crisis is most likely to occur (Erikson, 1956). During this phase, young people may feel overwhelmed by simultaneous pressures to commit themselves to serious physical intimacy, to decisive occupational choice, to competition in college or in the job market, and to further self-definition within their peer group (Erikson, 1956). The result may be a temporary period of *identity diffusion* or *role confusion* characterized by inability or unwillingness to make lasting commitments on any of these issues.

One kind of parental relationship appears to be especially difficult for adolescents. In that situation, one parent is unable to let go of the child and often intrudes deeply into the offspring's life, while the other parent is passive and unable or unwilling to establish a strong relationship with the child. Under these conditions, clinical evidence indicates that identity diffusion may become particularly severe (Erikson, 1956), interfering with the individual's perspective on time, ability to engage in intimate relationships, and ability to work. Even in such severe cases, what takes place during identity diffusion may be a relatively adaptive effort to deal with a difficult position (Erikson, 1956). Some young people choose a *negative identity*—the antithesis of everything their parents or societies insist they should be—as the only way out of a situation in which no truly personalized choices seem possible.

Erikson's notion of late adolescence as a *psychosocial moratorium,* a period during which societies allow young people to experiment with different roles and value systems, seems more applicable to the lives of college-going than non-college-going adolescents. On the other hand, his notion of identity crisis as a response to simultaneous pressures in the domains of physical intimacy, occupational commitment, competition, and self-definition seems applicable to all late adolescents. Unfortunately, very little is known about psychosocial moratoria and identity crises in the lives of young working people. Most of the available research has been conducted with college youth.

The freshman year of college seems to be a time of great fluctuation in identity status (Waterman & Waterman, 1971). Young men who begin college knowing what kind of career they want may be completely unsure by the end of that year. Conversely, youth who begin college not even wanting to think about a career may have made a choice before the year is out, although the stability of this choice is another question. Values and ideological commitments in the areas of religion and politics seem to be equally unstable during the freshman year. Academic difficulties related to these identity problems result in many students changing majors, changing schools, or dropping out of school altogether (Waterman & Waterman, 1972).

There seems to be an increase, although it is by no means steady and consistent, in the number of males who have achieved a firm sense of individual identity by their senior year of college (Constantinople, 1969, 1970; Waterman, Geary, & Waterman, 1974). However, there are also substantial numbers of men who are characterized by identity diffusion at the end of college (Waterman, Geary, & Waterman, 1974). The number of females characterized by identity diffusion may increase between freshman and senior years (Constantinople, 1969, 1970).

These findings should not be surprising. College probably constitutes an institutionalized form of the psychosocial moratorium for many young people. They go off to college expressly to find themselves, to learn, and to grow. However, young people encounter several very different kinds of college experiences. College may increase the range of choices available for consideration, but frequently there may be little in the college experience to help some individuals make those choices. Certainly four more years of "growing up" in college does not guarantee the achievement of identity. At the same time, it may be precisely the experience of college that frees some individuals from "psychosocial foreclosure."

Identity Statuses

The term *psychosocial foreclosure* raises an important issue concerning the theory and investigation of identity. Erikson (1956) makes only passing reference to the concept and does not define it clearly. What he implies is that individuals who "foreclose" on their identity development fail to confront the challenges and choices that lead, during adolescence, to a sense of personal identity and readiness for adult roles.

Investigators (Marcia and his associates) who have tried to operationalize, or to measure and study, Erikson's notions of identity have somewhat changed the definition of *identity foreclosure*. They have used two criteria to classify college students according to their identity status: the criteria of crisis and of commitment. The idea of crisis is, of course, a basic concept in Erikson's theory. It is a psychosocial crisis—for example, industry versus inferiority or identity versus role diffusion—that identifies or even defines each of the stages of development. For Erikson, the confrontation of and resolution of each crisis is largely an unconscious process. However, in their effort to examine the concept of crisis, Marcia and others have largely defined the *conscious* properties of crisis and confrontation. They focus on the active questioning of alternatives in relation to ideological (political, religious, or sexual) and vocational choice. *Commitment* refers to a relatively set investment in a course of action or set of values related to ideology or vocation.

Using these two criteria, Marcia and his associates have arrived at four or five distinct identity statuses. *Identity achievement* is characteristic of individuals who have undergone a period of crisis before making their commitments. *Identity diffusion* applies to individuals who, with or without undergoing any kind of crisis, remain uncommitted to anything and unwilling, or unable, to engage in any active search among alternatives. To this classification, some of Marcia's colleagues have added a subcategory of *alienated identity*. *Identity moratorium* refers to individuals who are currently in crisis and seeking commitments. *Identity foreclosure* refers to individuals who have made commitments but do not acknowledge having experienced a crisis.

This four-way classification of identity statuses clearly does some violence to Erikson's identity versus identity diffusion polarity. Moreover, inherent in the classification is the assumption that "crisis" must be conscious, which is not intrinsic to the original theory. Erikson (1960) has argued that, in some adolescents, in some cultures, and in some historical epochs, the identity crisis is minimal. He is not saying that all these adolescents are foreclosures. Indeed, he seems to think that the identity achieved with little crisis or identity consciousness in simpler societies may be much healthier than the complex, diffuse, standardizing, and conformity-inducing identity that is imposed on and accepted by youth in our society.

Despite these departures from Eriksonian theory, Marcia and his associates seem to have identified, at least within the context of North American society, meaningful dimensions of the identity experience. Individuals within each of the identity-status categories behave differently from one another. Moreover, the identity statuses seem to have different meanings and implications for females than they do for males, which is consistent with the assumption (Douvan & Adelson, 1966) that there are two identity crises—one for boys and one for girls. Let us look now at the picture of late adolescent identity development that emerges in the empirical literature.

Studies done with male and female college students in the late 1960s (Marcia & Friedman, 1970; Schenkel & Marcia, 1972) indicated that females were less likely than males to experience either crisis or commitment in relation to religion, politics, and occupation. However, the issue of premarital intercourse proved salient for women, and their sense of crisis and commitment over their own sexual behavior provided reliable grounds for categorizing them into the four identity statuses of moratorium, achievement, diffusion, and foreclosure.

More recent studies have indicated that, while college females may be more likely than males to experience a crisis over premarital intercourse, they may be no less likely to experience a crisis over occupation and ideology as well (Nevid, Nevid, O'Neill, & Waterman, 1974). In fact, different patterns of response to the identity crisis may be very much a function of the particular cultural group and era to which individuals belong. Whereas one-third of a sample of college women in Buffalo, New York, were classified as "foreclosures" on the basis of interviews concerning crisis and commitment over sex, religion, occupation, and politics (Schenkel & Marcia, 1972), only one-fifth of a comparable sample from a Boston-area college could be classified in that category (Schenkel, 1975). Reflecting, perhaps, a generational factor, male college students show a different pattern of ego identity statuses than do their own fathers. Fathers are significantly more likely than their sons to be classified into the foreclosure category and significantly less likely than their sons to be in the moratorium and diffusion statuses (Waterman & Waterman, 1975). Among the fathers, high levels of education seem to be related to identity achievement and low levels of education to identity diffusion. There does not seem to be any relationship between the identity statuses of fathers and sons (Waterman & Waterman, 1975).

What difference do these identity statuses make? Female college students who have achieved a sense of personal identity seem to be better able than other women to resist group pressures that go against their own judgments (Toder & Marcia, 1973). Young women who are in a state of role confusion, or identity diffusion, tend to be more conforming in group pressure situations than do women still experiencing a psychological moratorium. Interestingly enough, women in the foreclosed identity status, who have commitments without having gone through any crisis, seem more like identity achievers in their ability to resist certain pressures. Moreover, young women with foreclosed identities, like those who have achieved identities, seem more sure of their place in society and less ready to identify with deviant groups than women experiencing identity crises or diffusion. It is possible that within our society the foreclosure identity status provides as much ego strength and self-confidence to females as does identity achievement, simply because it represents the norm for women (Toder & Marcia, 1973). At any rate, college women classified as "foreclosures" are higher in self-esteem than any other group (Marcia & Friedman, 1970).

The effect of having arrived at commitments without having gone through a crisis may be different for males than it is for females. College women in the identity-foreclosure status have shown themselves capable of resisting certain kinds of conformity pressures, at least within the confines of a psychological laboratory. College men in the identity-foreclosure status seem in general to be highly conforming. Whereas men who have achieved an identity tend to reject authoritarian values ("My country right or wrong . . . "), foreclosed youths tend to endorse such values (Marcia, 1966, 1967). Foreclosed men also espouse a law-and-order type of morality (Podd, 1972). By contrast, men who have achieved their own identities have a good understanding of what are considered to be more "advanced" moral orientations; that is, they may have a commitment to principles of social contract ("Men make laws and change laws in accord with the common good"), or to universal moral codes ("Do unto others . . . ").

To move beyond the issue of conformity and consider the effects of identity development on other types of social interactions, there is some evidence that predictions can be made, on the basis of a young man's identity status, about his relationships with individuals of the opposite sex (Orlofsky, Marcia, & Lesser, 1973). College men who have achieved an identity are more likely than other young men to enter into mature—that is, close and sharing—and intimate relationships. Men who can be classified into foreclosure or diffusion identity statuses are more likely to lack deep relationships and genuine closeness with women. Foreclosed men, perhaps showing another kind of social conformity, are apt to be exploitive, using women as sex objects. Some of the young men who have resolved their identity crises in the negative direction of identity diffusion are complete isolates, with no close friends and no dating experience. Young men who are still experiencing a psychosocial moratorium are generally, like those who have achieved identity, ready to move into nonexploitive, mutual relationships. There have been no studies made of the relationship between identity status and participation in intimate relationships in women.

Academic Expectations and Performance

Level of identity development is related both to how well one does in school (Waterman & Waterman, 1972) and to how one feels about school. Freshman males who enter college with higher levels of identity development generally expect more from college than do their peers with a less well-established sense of identity (Waterman & Waterman, 1972). There is also evidence that, during their freshman year, females are significantly happier with college than are males (Constantinople, 1970). While both males and females show some increase in identity development between their freshman and senior years, it is only the males who show increased satisfaction with school (Constantinople, 1970). It may be that, while the males feel that they will be able to "go somewhere" with their sense of identity after college, females are less secure about the kind of life for which they are being prepared.

Clearly, the implications of identity status for behavior have had only the most minimal exploration. We believe that these implications are better described by adolescents themselves than by the skimpy research literature. Consider what this college male says about his apolitical behavior during his moratorium period:

> I would say that throughout adolescence I was almost completely apolitical. I had too much on my mind to be concerned with the world situation. Generally, as I got things settled in my own mind, I began to incorporate my ideas into more political, social, and cultural terms.
>
> I began to put some of these ideas into practice by doing volunteer work with children, talking more in class, explaining my feelings to others, and working on a political campaign or two. But, previously, I believed I could be of no help to others if I was muddled up inside of me—and I still think I was right.

Vocational Identity

As noted in Chapter Two, both Erikson and Piaget see vocational commitment as one criterion that marks the end of adolescence. However, vocational commitment—not a sudden accomplishment—is itself the outcome of a long developmental process. Indeed, the achievement of occupational identity can be seen as a component of the more general process of identity development.

Like identity development in general, vocational choice seems to have important unconscious elements stemming from experiences that go back to early childhood (Hackman & Davis, 1973; Nachmann, 1960). Moreover, if earlier psychosocial crises are not resolved satisfactorily, the individual may have difficulty making a vocational choice. Many people who seek counseling because of vocational identity problems report an absence of *trust* in themselves and their abilities or problems with *initiative* and *industry* (Galinsky & Fast, 1966). All of these are reflective of childhood psychosocial crises, as described by Erikson.

A number of investigators (see, for example, Borow, 1973) have tried to identify and describe major phases in the development of occupational identity. The adolescent years are seen as important both to the integration of personal interests, aptitudes, values, and education with personal goals (Ginzberg, 1972) and to the acquisition of basic work habits through homework, chores, and part-time work (Havighurst, 1964). Serious vocational commitments, or crises over commitments, usually do not become a real issue until late adolescence. College may serve both to broaden the individual's choices for a life's work (Coons, 1970) and to increase the likelihood of identity self-consciousness over the issue of vocational identity. Many individuals, like Erikson, either delay making firm vocational commitments until they are well into their twenties or make one or two "midcareer" changes as they continue, into the adult years, to explore the possibilities within their own identities.

Other major criteria marking the end of adolescence are the development of a personal ethic and the achievement of a mature and intimate relationship with a member of the opposite sex. Both of these achievements, like mature thought and identity, reflect life-long developmental processes. In Chapters Five and Six, we will consider moral development and psychosexual-identity development, particularly as these reflect the crises and achievements of the adolescent years.

Chapter Five

Moral Judgment and Values

Much of my present attitudes had been set by age 16, a mature 16 it was. I despised religion. It sucked then, and it holds little for me now. I didn't really have a morally conscious attitude at 16 (as you may have guessed, a clear age for me, senior year in high school) and I know I do now. By 16 I was into girls, figuratively and literally. I enjoyed sex then and I enjoy it even more now. One difference: at 16, any chick would do. At 20, I have developed an unfortunately morally conscious attitude which says one woman at a time.

My political inclinations were really together. In 1964, at 12, I was a Robert Kennedy man. By 1965, I had gotten into verbally attacking anyone who spoke in favor of the Vietnam bar-b-que. By the age of 15, I was selling the High School Free Press, and dug getting busted and sent to the Dean's office. By the time I got to college I was tired of beating my head against the wall. Bobby Kennedy was dead and Gene McCarthy had proven what a fruit he was. And Richard Nixon was President—oh, woe is us. Went to a couple of demos for the vibes and just hung out other times. Despair.

We have seen that adolescence is the time when the individual becomes capable of dealing with the abstract and the purely hypothetical. It is also the time during which one either grapples with or avoids the issue of who one is and where one is going. During adolescence, the individual may begin to structure, evaluate, interpret, define, and apply a personal code of ethics. Although the behavior of the young child can be seen in moral terms and although children themselves may label their own behavior as good or bad, it probably is not until adolescence that individuals can become moral philosophers in their own right.

Psychologists have been concerned with at least three different aspects of moral development: moral behavior, moral feelings, and moral judgment. Moral behavior refers to what we actually do in a situation of moral decision. Moral feelings, such as guilt, consist of our emotional reactions to our own behavior in situations that have ethical implications. Moral judgment refers to our interpretation of moral rules and our evaluation of the kinds of behaviors and resolutions likely to be associated with moral conflicts. Moral judgment, moral behavior, and moral feelings do not always coincide; that is, we do not always behave in ways that are completely consistent with our own judgment of what the "correct" or most ethical behavior is. Moreover, we may or may not feel guilty about what we have done in a situation, even if we judge that different behavior would have been more appropriate.

While moral judgments are not the same as specific cultural values ("A penny saved is a penny earned"), they are related to broader sets of values concerning the good and the desirable in life. It is with the development of moral judgments and values that we will be concerned in this chapter.

Piaget and Kohlberg look at moral judgment in the context of theories of cognitive development. From this point of view, children's moral judgments are, at least in part, a function of their developmental stage. Cross-cultural differences in predominant moral codes to a certain degree reflect the extent to which cognitive development is facilitated or retarded in different societies or social groups.[1] Both Piaget and Kohlberg recognize the impact of social learning—which involves observing and behaving like adult models and responding to rewards and punishments—on the content of some aspects of moral values. However, both also surmise that certain universal features exist in moral judgments, reflecting a basis in general human development.

Piaget (1965) describes "two moralities" or phases of development that correspond roughly to the stages of concrete and formal operations. The morality of the child, called "moral realism" by Piaget, is heteronomous—that is, imposed by adults. Goodness consists of obedience to rules, and it is the letter rather than the spirit of the law that is important. Badness is linked to the objective magnitude of an act: it is worse to break ten cups by accident than one on purpose. Justice consists of punishment and retribution for misdeeds.

When a child is about 12 years old, the morality of adult constraint is replaced by a morality of cooperation, and heteronomy is replaced by autonomy. Unlike the young child, the adolescent can conceive of rules whose validity derives not from a unilateral respect for adult authority but from the mutual respect and reciprocity of peers. As adolescents become capable of understanding motives, badness becomes linked to intent. It is no longer what you do but why you do it that determines how you should be judged. Justice consists of equalitarianism combined with equity, or democ-

---

[1] For a critique of these assumptions, see Simpson (1974).

racy tempered with a greater tolerance for the unfortunate and the disadvantaged.

In a more articulated developmental theory of moral judgment, Kohlberg (1963) postulates a series of qualitatively distinct and hierarchically related stages that follow each other in an invariant sequence. He classifies the stages of moral development into three broad levels: preconventional, conventional, and postconventional, or principled. Preadolescents generally are on the preconventional level, in which right and wrong are defined in terms of the physical consequences of punishment and reward or in terms of the physical powers of the rule-givers, as in "Might makes right." More typical of adolescence is the conventional level, in which right consists of conformity to the expectations of the family, social milieu, or nation and in the maintenance of these groups and their norms. Finally, on the postconventional level, which may begin to emerge in late adolescence, good becomes dependent on a set of moral principles that have validity independent of the particular social groups to which the individual belongs.

Each of these three levels consists of two substages, making a total of six substages of moral development. The individual has a different orientation toward morality in each of these stages. We first will describe these stages and then indicate the approximate ages at which they emerge in the North American middle-class individual. Stage 1, at the preconventional level, is characterized by a punishment-and-obedience orientation. Good consists of obedience and the avoidance of punishment. Stage 2, also at the preconventional level, is characterized by a hedonistic relativity: "If I like it, it's good." Good is that which satisfies one's own needs, either directly or indirectly, through satisfying the needs of others: "I'll scratch your back if you'll scratch mine." At the conventional level, Stage 3 is defined by a "good boy—nice girl" orientation. Good is that which pleases or helps others and is approved of by them. Stage 4, still at the conventional level, is defined by a law-and-order orientation. Good consists of doing one's duty, respecting authority, and maintaining the social order of one's own community: if it's against the law for Black people to ride in the front of the bus, then it's also immoral for them to do so. Stage 5, or the early principled stage, marks the achievement of a social contract, a constitutional orientation. Good is defined by consensus. It is arrived at by democratic principles and is subject to revision. An example of this is: any law that discriminates against individuals is a violation of the Constitution and should be abandoned. Stage 6, or the late principled stage, represents the achievement of a universal ethical orientation. Good is a matter of individual conscience operating on the basis of abstract and autonomously selected ethical principles: any law that discriminates against my brother is a violation of higher principles and should be resisted. Ethical principles, exemplified by the Golden Rule and the categorical imperative, are comprehensive, universal, and mutually consistent.

Kohlberg and his associates have carried out a number of studies of the development of moral judgment in adolescents and young adults, usually male. Using a technique similar to Piaget's (1965), Kohlberg (1973) determines the subject's stage of moral development on the basis of the response to questions involving moral dilemmas that are presented in story form. He reports that moral-judgment responses classifiable at Stage 1 and Stage 2, or the preconventional level, decrease rapidly during early adolescence, while responses at Stage 3 and Stage 4, or the conventional level, increase during this time. Not until middle and late adolescence do young people begin to make a substantial number of responses classifiable at the Stage 5, or early principled, level. Even in the mid-20s, Stage 6 responses are notably rare.

It seems to be an exposure to diverse points of view that encourages the breakdown of conventional thinking and the emergence of postconventional thinking in late adolescence. The complacency of law-and-order thinking seems first to give way to inconsistency, conflict, and internal contradiction (Turiel, 1974). At the end of high school and during the early college years, many students fall into an inconsistent moral relativism; that is, they insist that all moral values are arbitrary (so, "When in Rome . . ."), while maintaining commitment to specific moral positions such as "Life is always more valuable than property." While such students show a real understanding of the value of individual freedom, they also show a tremendous confusion over what is moral and what is just social convention (Turiel, 1974).

When an individual reaches the age of 25, much of this "Stage 4½" (Kohlberg, 1973) confusion and relativism is resolved—either backward in the direction of law and order or forward in the direction of an emphasis on broad, democratic-constitutional principles. Thus, while college seems to contribute to the examination of prior assumptions in many youth, the ethical confusion is by no means always resolved in favor of the "higher level" (more flexible and tolerant) orientation. On the other hand, Kohlberg reports that none of the subjects whom he studied longitudinally developed principled thinking if they went directly into the Army and/or adult occupations instead of to college. He concludes that movement from conventional to postconventional thought requires both personal experiences of choice involving questioning and commitment and the kind of stimulation to reflect on moral and cognitive issues that often is found in college.

Kohlberg's views of the process involved in the development of postconventional thought are quite congruent with Erikson's views of identity development. That is, questioning and commitment are major processes in the achievement of identity.

> Late adolescence was and still is a time of internal struggle. For me, there was never an active and vociferous period of rebellion against parents and authority figures. It seems that during this period the values that have been passed on from parents must be examined and separated, some to be adopted and others to be discarded. Again, sex is an issue, only now in a different context. Political and religious beliefs are also examined, discarded, or reincorporated. This period seems to be one in which I have sought some sort of internal judgment and justification for my actions and beliefs, with worry for approval from parents and peers still important but decreasingly so. Also, decision making becomes crucial as I must now decide what I shall do with a life that has for so many years been geared exclusively towards going to college as its main goal, with an occasional fleeting glance beyond.

Sociopolitical Judgments

The basic assumption in Kohlberg's and Piaget's theories of cognitive development is that the judgments of adolescents should be qualitatively different from those of younger children. It's not just a matter of more values or more strongly held values. It's not even just a matter of more complex and more differentiated values (see Webster, 1958). It's a matter of reasoning about issues of ethics or values in ways that are qualitatively different from before—approaching problems from newly evolved perspectives and coming to conclusions on the basis of newly embraced principles.

How are theoretical constructs manifested in the judgments that adolescents make about real and hypothetical situations? In one type of study, subjects are asked to imagine that a thousand men and women, dissatisfied with the way things are going in their country, decide to purchase and move to a remote island in the Pacific. Questions centering on a wide range of dilemmas that could arise in this situation—for example "Would the people have to have laws?"—are posed to children and to adolescents. Attempts to deal with these dilemmas can reveal a great deal about the youths' value systems and sociopolitical-ethical judgments.

When presented with this kind of problem, adolescents of 11 to 13 years emphasize the coercive side of law (Adelson, Green, & O'Neil, 1969). Such youngsters believe that laws are essential, that laws should be obeyed at all costs, and that authorities must be respected without question. This "moralistic" orientation begins to give way to greater political realism between the ages of 13 and 15, as young people come to realize that authorities *can* and sometimes, unfortunately, do misuse power.

The age of 15 seems to be a major turning point in the individual's development of ideas about law (Adelson, Green, & O'Neil, 1969). Before they are 15, adolescents tend to view laws in a black-or-white fashion— either they are necessary and should be strengthened completely and enforced absolutely, or they are unnecessary and should be abolished. After the age of 15, adolescents show a sudden sense of community. Laws are then seen as amendable contracts designed to serve the needs of the members of the community. The beneficial rather than the coercive aspects of law become emphasized.

Changes in the adolescent's notions of law take place along with other changes in thought. Indeed, the overall understanding of the social and political community and the relationship of community to individual seem to undergo important transformations during adolescence. Children aged 11 generally have an egocentric view, in Piaget's sense, of the community (Adelson & O'Neil, 1966). If they are asked about the role of government in life, they frequently answer with personal pronouns, referring to the government as "he" ("He fixes roads" and "He makes people obey"). Their understanding of political and legal processes is concrete and personal. A government is good if "he" safeguards them from the evil intents of others.

These changes in views and values begin to emerge in an individual by the age of 13. There begins to be an understanding of government as a complex whole instead of as a series of isolated functions, like the construction of roads and the collection of taxes. There is some recognition that communities have a future that extends beyond the lives of its current inhabitants and that today's political decisions can affect the citizens of tomorrow. An orientation also develops toward considering not only the personal and social consequences of a given action but also its ethical implications. For example, while many older adolescents recognize the personal and social benefits that might accrue from requiring all men over 45 years of age to have a yearly physical examination, some of these adolescents still oppose such a law because of its infringement on personal freedom.

Adelson and O'Neil (1966) argue that the kinds of responses adolescents make to questions about the imaginary island community show that Piagetian formal operations are established firmly in them by the age of 15. That is, by 15, young people show an ability to deal with the purely hypothetical in abstract terms and to deduce possibilities from general principles. It can be argued that these youth also are showing Kohlbergian principled, or postconventional, thinking. They view laws as changeable rather than immutable, fallible rather than perfect, and as people-oriented rather than authority-given products of the democratic process.

Despite the evidence that after early adolescence youth become less authoritarian and more aware of rules as modifiable prescriptions guiding social life, it should not be assumed that all adolescents become steadfast defenders of human rights and freedom. While some North American youth describe ideal legal systems in highly ethical and universal terms, many only sloganize, showing a conventional rule-maintaining orientation (Tapp & Levine, 1972). It seems likely that one's choice of a morality of law and order or a morality of dissent reflects not only one's cognitive capacities but also the particular groups, conforming or radical, in which one's ongoing socialization takes place.

As a result of Tapp's investigations of legal socialization, Tapp and Kohlberg (1971) have formulated a model of the development of political thinking that corresponds in major ways to Kohlberg's model of moral development. In Tapp's scheme, a Level I view of laws, which corresponds to preconventional thinking and is typical in elementary school, emphasizes the punitive and prohibitive role of laws. Children at this stage obey in order to avoid punishment or in submission to superior power. They regard laws as immutable and unbreakable.

Law-obeying thinking gives way to law-maintaining thinking by the time youth reach junior high school. This Level II, or conventional, legal reasoning is characterized by a prescriptive view of law. Level II youth follow rules in order to conform socially. In their view, laws can be changed or broken if doing so results in greater kindness or greater social conformity.

Finally, Level III, or postconventional, legal reasoning emphasizes the beneficial aspects of law. Laws are seen by youth at this level as being the products of reason and principled judgments. Laws can be changed or broken when they are immoral or unjust. Adolescents and adults at Level III are no longer law-obeyers or law-maintainers. They are law-makers. However, as is the case with principled moral judgment, postconventional legal reasoning is not the norm even in college (Tapp & Kohlberg, 1971).

The relationship between political and moral judgment is not just speculative. Indeed, moral judgment seems to be related not only to political judgment but also to political behavior. Haan, Smith, and Block (1968) obtained answers to several of Kohlberg's moral dilemma stories from over 200 students who took part in the well-known sit-in for freedom of speech at Berkeley. It was determined, from the total sample of respondents, how many students from each moral-judgment category had been arrested for civil disobedience. Eighty percent of the students who had reached Stage 6, or principled, morality were among those arrested, along with about 50% of the Stage 5, or social-contract students. Only about 20% of the students who were at a conventional, or Stage 4, level of morality were in the arrested group.

In another look at the same data (Block, Haan, & Smith, 1973), it was found that the majority of all the protestors (at least 56%) were at the postconventional level of morality. Among the nonprotestors, only 12% were at this level. Conversely, 85% of the nonprotestors were in the conventional stages of morality, and only 36% of the protestors were in that stage. Thus, it looks as if many principled thinkers are willing to act on their principles.

> In 1960 I supported Nixon for President. My support was very active, as I worked for an average of an hour or more a day in the local campaign headquarters. I became known to a great many of the local Republican leaders. In some ways this can be seen as a reflection of my parents' political views. I see it also as a desire on my part to be active and engaged in the action. As a child one of my fondest hobbies was reading English and American history, often concerning my mother by spending time with books instead of playing. I developed a set of values that placed the individual's rights at the highest point of value. At the early teen period I saw the conservative view as coming closest to these ideals and accepted that liberalism and communism were on the side of the state. Very much a William Buckley position. It was with my move to Cambridge that I began to challenge this position and find that my values were on the left of the spectrum. The activism of earlier times continued and the end of adolescence found me politically active and happy with myself for the first time.

Achievement Judgments

Although advanced levels of thinking may free youth to think in hypothetical and universal terms, many of the issues about which they are asked to reflect—both in real life and in the psychological laboratory—are concrete and culturally defined. For example, achievement is a highly valued concept in Western society. How does the evaluation of achievement develop?

Achievement judgments can be elicited in approximately the same way as moral judgments can—by presenting an issue in story form and asking for evaluations of various aspects of the situation. In our culture, issues of achievement generally focus on two components: effort and outcome. Younger children rate objective outcome in an achievement situation, as they do in moral judgments, as being more important than any subjective considerations, such as effort (Weiner & Peter, 1973). This relationship is reversed at the onset of puberty at 10 to 12 years of age, but older adolescents rate outcome as the thing that counts, although the role of effort is still considered to be important. This valuing of outcome by American youth may represent a predominant influence of socialization over developing cognitive flexibility. That is, adolescents recognize that, however much "lip service" may be given to the glories of hard work, in reality it is successful achievement that pays off and therefore is "valuable." It may be exactly this kind of pragmatism, fostered in American society, that accounts for the low percentages of individuals making moral judgments that can be characterized as postconventional.

Also important to achievement judgments is the amount of ability that the individual brings to the situation. With development, children become increasingly lenient in their evaluation of story characters who are portrayed as lacking in ability. However, a well-articulated notion of a compensatory relationship between ability and effort does not emerge clearly in adolescents before the ages of 16 to 18 (Weiner & Peter, 1973).

Religion is also an issue with which many adolescents must deal. Starbuck (Vetter & Green, 1932) reported finding that 90% of all people who converted to religions did so between the ages of 10 and 20 years. Most conversions to atheism, by contrast, occurred after the age of 20. In Vetter and Green's sample, the age of 15 seemed to be a crucial one for members of the American Association for the Advancement of Atheists. While 90% of these atheists reported having attended church or Sunday School before the age of 15, only 61% attended after they were 15—and only 25% of these went willingly.

The decline of authoritarianism in political beliefs is accompanied by a similar phenomenon in the area of religious beliefs. While many 12-year-olds are ready to believe statements like "every word in the Bible is true," many fewer 18-year-olds are willing to accept such statements (Kuhlen & Arnold, 1944). As this authoritarianism declines, tolerance increases; more 18-year-olds than 12-year-olds are willing to agree that Catholics, Jews, and Protestants are all equally "good."

There are, of course, individual differences in these developmental trends. Some adolescents are more authoritarian than others. There does seem to be some consistency among an individual's values, however. Adolescents who adopt a strict and conservative position on going to church and reading the Bible are likely to adopt a similarly strict position on smoking, lying, and stealing (Wright & Cox, 1967). Thus, as might be expected, adolescents who consider themselves to be religious tend to be morally stricter than adolescents who do not. In England, at least, girls seem to be more severe than boys in many of their religious and moral judgments, and girls in single-sex schools tend to be more severe, particularly regarding smoking and premarital sex, than girls in coed schools (Wright & Cox, 1967).

Logic

The adolescent who has achieved fully developed formal operations can deal with the purely hypothetical. Since such adolescents can go beyond the immediate context in physical problem solving, it would not be surprising if they could think beyond the laws and mores of their own social groups in considering moral issues. Consequently, one would expect that the advanced formal-operational thinker would be capable of postconventional moral judgments. If it is true that formal-operational thinking is relatively rare in adolescents and adults, then it follows that principled thinking would also be relatively rare.

Reasoning in this way, Tomlinson-Keasey and Keasey (1974) looked at the relationship between cognitive and moral development in 30 sixth-grade girls and 24 college coeds. Performances on six of Kohlberg's moral dilemma stories and three of Piaget's formal-operational tasks were examined. The eight coeds who showed formal-operational thinking on all of the Piagetian tasks showed postconventional thinking in over 40% of their responses to the moral dilemmas. Coeds who demonstrated less formal-operational thinking also showed less principled thinking. There was little formal-operational thinking in the sixth-grade girls and even less principled thinking. The consistent "lag" between the cognitive and moral levels supported the notion that formal operations are necessary but not sufficient for postconventional thinking. The findings of Lee (1971) with preadolescent and adolescent boys are consistent with this pattern. Also consistent are the findings of Kuhn, Langer, Kohlberg, and Haan (unpublished study) with subjects ranging in age from 10 to 50 years and those of Black (1974) with subjects aged 9 to 35 years.

We have already noted that the most advanced thinking demonstrated on the "imaginary island" sociopolitical task might reflect a high level of cognitive development. It is also possible that both sociopolitical judgment and moral judgment are specialized applications of cognitive operations. However, as pointed out in Chapter Three, one's level of cognitive functioning is at least partially dependent on the content of the assessment task. The same individual may show formal operations on Piaget's pendulum task but only concrete operations on the balance task. Maybe the same type of "lag" is operating when a youth shows formal operations on the balance task but only conventional thinking in a moral dilemma.

In one relevant study, Kuhn, Langer, Kohlberg, and Haan (unpublished study) administered Piagetian cognitive tasks, Kohlbergian moral judgment dilemmas, and a social-order ("imaginary island") task to 162 individuals from four age groups (10 to 15, 16 to 20, 21 to 30, and 45 to 50). The social-order task, adapted from Adelson and O'Neil (1966), was scored for developmental stage using criteria similar in form to those used for assessing stage in Kohlberg's tasks.

Kuhn et al. found that 75% of the adolescents and adults who achieved the highest level of thinking on the cognitive task were also at the highest level on the social-order task. Stage levels on the social-order and the cognitive tasks were more closely related to each other than either was to stage level on the moral judgment task. On the basis of their data, Kuhn et al. suggest that advanced thinking is mastered by adolescents in the following sequence: (1) formal operations in the purely logical domain; (2) formal operations (or principled-level thought) in the conception of the social order; (3) comprehension of principled judgments in the moral domain; and (4) spontaneous use of principled moral judgments in the solution of moral dilemmas.

Identity

Our expectations about the relationship between cognitive development and the level of moral judgment have received some confirmation. Adolescents who use principled moral judgment are likely to be in the formal-operational stage of cognitive development. Adolescents who use conventional moral judgment already may have reached formal operations or still may be in the concrete-operational stage. Adolescents who use preconventional moral judgment are likely to be still in the concrete-operational stage.

Thus far in this chapter, we have emphasized the relationships between logical and moral development. However, we assume that there is also a relationship between moral judgment and social-emotional development as described by Erikson. What kinds of correspondences might be expected? It seems unlikely that the group of adolescents described by Marcia as "identity foreclosures" would reason in postconventional ways. Individuals who have foreclosed on their identities accept with little apparent questioning their parents' view of who they should be. This kind of acceptance would seem to fit more comfortably with a conventional good boy/nice girl or law-and-order view of morality than with a universal orientation.

Adolescents who have not yet resolved the identity crisis might be expected to be in the transitional stage between conventional and postconventional levels of thought. The kind of confusion that they feel about themselves and their place in the world might very well extend to a confusion about relativity and universality in ethical principles.

Adolescents who have achieved a stable ego identity are the ones most likely to have achieved principled moral judgment. They have wrestled with the problem of who they are and where they are going and have attained a perspective that extends beyond their families and immediate social groups. Their ability to consider and then choose among alternative "selves" and roles might very well be accompanied by a consideration of alternative moral codes, a flirtation with complete ethical relativity, and a resolution of moral conflict in favor of a social contract or universal code.

Finally, there are the adolescents who do not resolve their identity conflicts positively but remain in a state of identity diffusion. It seems unlikely that these adolescents, who cannot commit themselves to a stable identity or to a set of life roles, can commit themselves to a universal or democratic moral code. It is even questionable whether they would commit themselves to the code of conventional morality. Rather, it would seem likely that the adolescent manifesting identity diffusion would operate at the preconventional level of reward and punishment or of self-gratification.

These speculations are not only theoretically elegant but are also supported empirically. Although there is not much research relevant to the issue, we did find one study. Podd (1972) examined the relationship between levels of moral development and identity status in 112 male college juniors and seniors. The pattern of relationships that was found conformed substantially to the one that we just outlined.

Role Taking

Kohlberg has argued (1969) that moral development is essentially a process of transformations in forms of role taking. His view is roughly as follows:

The relationships of a child or an adolescent in the preconventional stage of morality reflect an unequal distribution of power and an "egocentric," nonmutual barter for goods. The Stage 1 child trades off obedience for freedom from punishment. The relationships of Stage 2 individuals are characterized by another kind of nonmutual trade-off in which each simply does whatever has to be done to achieve purely personal pleasure.

Conventional-level adolescents and adults engage in role relationships that are characterized by greater reciprocity and mutuality. These adolescents share the assumption that, if everyone conforms to the expectations of the family (Stage 3) or of the broader social group (Stage 4), everyone will be happy and life will be secure. For the postconventional adolescent and adult, role relationships are defined by either a flexible social contract, wherein the rights of life, liberty, and the pursuit of happiness are guaranteed to all people, or a universal moral code, by which one will "do unto others. . . . "

If Kohlberg is correct in his analysis, there should be an intimate correspondence between one's ability to enter into mature relationships of give-and-take and one's ability to reason about moral issues. Both interpersonal relationships and moral judgments, with development, should reflect greater reciprocity and equality in their definitions of human relationships.

A greater ability to understand another's perspective does appear to be related to higher levels of moral judgment in preadolescents (Selman, 1971). Children who are unable to take the role of another tend to use preconventional moral thought. Children who can put themselves "in the shoes" of another are more likely to use conventional moral thought.

Tracy and Cross (1973) did not find this relationship between role taking and moral development in a sample of young (12- to 15-year-old) adolescents. However, if we consider delinquent and nondelinquent behaviors to reflect different levels of moral development, there is evidence that role taking and moral development are related in young adolescents. Chandler (1973) found that delinquents between the ages of 11 and 13 had serious deficits in role-taking ability as compared to nondelinquents. Remedial training in role taking not only improved this ability but also was followed by a significant reduction in delinquent behavior. Although the focus here is on a form of moral behavior rather than on moral judgments per se, Kohlberg and his associates assume that the two aspects of moral development bear some relationship to each other.

Socialization

Our discussion of the relationships of logic, identity, and role taking to moral development should not be interpreted in terms of cause-and-effect relationships. We have noted that the passing of time, or aging, does not cause changes in the level of moral judgment; neither do developments in logic, identity, and role taking cause changes in moral judgment. Rather, all of these developments represent the results of interactions between the organism and the environment, interactions that contribute to changes in all aspects of human functioning. The organism is a whole, and it should not be surprising that, when young people begin to understand hypothetical problems in science, they also begin thinking about alternative selves, alternative roles, alternative societies, and alternative ethics. Developments in all these spheres are interrelated because they all result from the interactions of the same organism.

Among the experiences that are important to human development are all those interactions contained in the word "socialization." Although this term has been used in different ways, its core meaning refers to the acquisition of behavior consistent with group norms and values. The role of reinforcement and modeling in this process frequently is emphasized by socialization researchers. However, we should not lose sight of the active tendency of children to structure their environment, to respond to reinforcement, and to adopt the behavior of parents because they have labeled themselves as "like Mommy" or "like Daddy" or as a "good girl" or a "good boy." Socialization is not a one-way process enforced on a completely passive youngster.

The primary socializers, because of their control over reinforcers and their availability as models, are family members—especially parents. Another socializing factor is the child's own tendency toward identification. We already have looked at the way a variety of family characteristics can affect development in cognitive and identity processes; it is reasonable to ask what kind of role the family plays in moral development. Unfortunately, the picture is, at this point, very incomplete.

Hoffman (1970, 1971a, 1971b; Hoffman & Saltzstein, 1967) has tried to prove that the level of moral judgment in pubescent children of 12 to 13 years of age is related to their parents' child-rearing techniques as well as to the children's own tendency to identify with one parent or the other. Identifying with parents is defined by Hoffman as admiring, wanting to be like, and seeing oneself as "taking after" one or the other of the parents. While it is likely that child-rearing techniques and identification do play a role in the development of moral judgment, Hoffman's portrayal of this role as occurring at the beginning of adolescence cannot be accepted uncritically. Writing before Kohlberg's more recent formulations of moral judgment theory, Hoffman compares the upbringing of what he calls "postconventional" with "conventional" thinking in middle-class and lower-class pubescent youths. Strict Kohlbergians would not accept the assumption that any of these early adolescents had achieved postconventional thinking. To them, judgments even at Stage 4, the conventional level, would be expected to be rare among these adolescents.

Studies of the relationships of socialization factors to the level of moral judgments and values of college students are more promising. Even when investigations have been carried out before Kohlberg's reformulations were made, there is a basis for translating outmoded diagnoses of moral stage into the more current conceptualizations. Let's turn now to representative studies of the impact of socialization procedures on late-adolescent moral judgments, values, and behaviors.

We already have talked a little about college student activism. It should not be surprising to find that, not only were there differences in moral judgment between protestors and nonprotestors, but there were also differences in the ways that they had been reared. In a study of students from the University of California at Berkeley and from San Francisco State College, as well as in studies of Peace Corps volunteers, Block, Haan, and Smith (1969) identified five types of youth, who varied in political activism and social service. Let's consider first what these groups were like and then see how they differed in their reports about their parents.

There were, first of all, the "inactives," who took part in no political or social organizations or activities. There were also "conventionalists"—young men and women who were part of the fraternity/sorority world. In general, conventionalists showed little involvement in either political or social-service activities. Another major group were the "constructionists." These adolescents were very active in social service and less active in politics. Next there were the "dissenters." These students were politically active and politically dissident but not active in social-service commitments. Finally, there were the "activists," who were high in both political protests and social-service activities.

These groups reported different child-rearing histories and patterns of identification (Block, Haan, & Smith, 1969). The inactive students described their parents as concerned with conformity, obedience, and docility. The conventionalists reported a warm identification with parents who adhered to traditional social and political values. Constructivists offered a relatively positive evaluation of parents, whom they nevertheless viewed as being restrictive. Dissenters described their parents' socialization practices as lacking in coherence. These parents seemed to be indulgent and permissive but, at the same time, opposed to their children's need for privacy. Finally, the activists portrayed warm parents who encouraged independence and responsibility in accordance with inner-directed goals. These parents, like their children after them, were opposed to aggression and violence—not only in word but also in deed.

If students are classified simply according to the more traditional categories of rightist and leftist, or activist and inactivist, some differences in patterns of socialization and values still emerge. Students who are activists are more likely than nonactivist students to have parents who are also activists (Lewis & Kraut, 1972). Thus, it is a mistake to look at all student activism as a rebellion against the middle class or against "middle-American" values of parents. Quite to the contrary, many student activists simply are following in their parents' footsteps. Moreover, not all activists are leftist in political orientation. Political right-wingers as well as political left-wingers can be found among both active and inactive groups.

While rightists and leftists cannot be differentiated on the basis of activist versus nonactivist commitments, they can be differentiated on the basis of a variety of values. Many conservatives describe themselves as espousing the traditional work ethic of U. S. society (Lewis & Kraut, 1972). They are more sure of their futures and less open to new experiences than are their leftist counterparts. They describe their ideal selves as practical and conventional. By contrast, leftists describe themselves and their ideal selves as loving, humanistic, and independent. They are less likely than their right-wing peers to be religious.

The differences in perceived parental permissiveness that Block,

Smith, and Haan found in their Berkeley student groups may not be characteristic of all student groups. Lewis and Kraut (1972) found no differences among activists and inactivists or leftists and rightists in their accounts of parental upbringing techniques. However, for both activist and inactivist groups, the leftists reported significantly more conflicts with their parents than did the rightists. It may be that the leftists saw a greater discrepancy between their parents' professed values and their actual behavior than did the rightists. This could be true even if there were relatively high agreement between students and parents on political issues. In one study (Thomas, 1971) the average college student/parent agreement on 12 political issues was 75%. While the percentage of agreement was 77% for conservative activists and their parents and 70% for nonactivists and their parents, it rose to 90% for liberal activist students and their parents.

Socialization does not end with parents. Schools, peers, neighbors, churches, governments, the media, and other social groups share in the socialization process. The youth's choice of an occupation, a career, or a particular major in college reflects previous socialization. The new institutions with which he or she becomes involved continue the socialization process—although not always along the same lines as begun by the family. Ours is a diverse society, and, even within "middle America," there is some competition among norms and values. While children initially may identify with their parents, during adolescence they may come to identify themselves in different ways. They may think, for example, "I am a free thinker . . . a rebel . . . a budding social reformer . . . someone who can lead others back to the traditional ways." These new self-identifications can lead, in turn, to openness to new socialization pressures. Previously socialized to conservative norms and values, the farmer's son in college may become socialized to the norms of the "hippie."

The kinds of competing values and moral codes available on a college campus can be seen in a case study of 100 students, 60 faculty members, and 16 administrators at Yale University (Fontana & Noel, 1973). These representatives of three important campus groups completed a questionnaire packet that included Kohlberg stories, a political-ideology (left, right, middle) scale, and a political-activism scale. Interestingly enough, it was not the overall group role of student, faculty, or administrator that was related most significantly to level of moral reasoning. That is, while administrators were more likely than students or faculty to use Stage 4, or law-and-order, thinking, students were not, contrary to expectation, more likely to use what Kohlberg calls Stage 4½ thinking. Similarly, faculty were not more likely to use postconventional thinking. There were no significant differences between students and faculty in level of moral reasoning.

Across all three role groups, individuals espousing a rightist ideology were highest in Stage 4 reasoning, while leftists were lowest. There was a significant correlation between leftist ideology and Stage 4½ reasoning, suggesting that individuals socialized to a leftist ideology were uncomfortable with a law-and-order morality. There was no relationship, however, between political ideology and the use of Stage 6 reasoning.

While there were only minimal differences in moral reasoning between activist and nonactivist students, activist faculty reasoned more at Stages 5 and 6 than did inactivist faculty. Inactive faculty reasoned more at Stage 4½. Natural scientists reasoned more at Stage 4 and less at Stage 5 than did social scientists and humanists. Among the administrators, middle-of-the-roaders reasoned more at Stage 5 and less at Stage 4 than did rightists. Younger administrators used Stage 5 more and Stage 4½ less than older administrators.

Sexuality and Sex Role

When people talk about what is moral and immoral, they frequently are referring to a broad variety of sexual behaviors. In fact, one could infer that almost all except a very narrowly defined and restricted set of sexual activities are immoral. The whole socialization process seems to play an important role in determining which behaviors will be labeled immoral. In our society, sex is "bad"; moreover, if you're a male, acting in an "unmasculine" way is reprehensible. Yet we know that neither sexual mores nor definitions of masculinity and femininity are universal, adding weight to the argument that moral judgments about specific sexual issues are arbitrary and culturally relative outcomes of the socialization process.

While the content of moral judgments about sexual behavior may be a product of socialization, the form of the judgments reflects the broader process of moral development. Attaching moral labels to any behavior, sexual or otherwise, that conforms to social expectations is, of course, one type of what Kohlberg called conventional-level thinking. The ability to separate sexual conventions and sex-role prescriptions from a reflective evaluation of the implications of specific behaviors for the greater good of the greater number (or some autonomously derived ethical principle) reflects achievement of postconventional moral judgment.

The level of adolescent judgments about sexual issues is generally consistent with their reasoning about standard Kohlberg dilemmas (Gilligan, Kohlberg, Lerner, & Belenky, 1971). However, a substantial proportion of adolescents seem to reason at a lower stage in regard to sexual issues than in regard to the standard dilemmas. Whether this represents a scoring problem, or the failure to identify Stage 4½ thinking, or whether it represents a real lag in the ability of adolescents to use their "best thinking" in dealing with sexual matters is as yet unclear.

At any rate, the whole area of sexual and sex-role development is complex enough to warrant more detailed consideration. In Chapter 6, we will see how cognitive, identity, and socialization factors interact in the development of the adolescent psychosexual identity.

Chapter Six

Sex Roles and Sexuality

In Junior High School, my interest in boys grew even greater. I "went steady" with another boy almost every other week. Even so, I was known as a "prude" for I would just make out, but I wouldn't let the boys "feel me up." Even with my popularity, my self-esteem was pretty weak. I was overly concerned with my appearance. I didn't like my freckles, thought my nose was much too large, and if it was windy, I would walk around holding my bangs down on my forehead because I thought I looked ugly without them.

One answer to the question "Who am I?" is "I am a girl becoming a woman" or "I am a boy becoming a man." This answer, though, brings no particular comfort to the growing individual and no definite resolution to an identity crisis. Nor are the adolescent's expanding cognitive capacities necessarily helpful in the process of clarifying a psychosexual identity. The ability to consider alternatives flexibly and to imagine purely hypothetical possibilities does not facilitate immediate resolution to an identity crisis focused on sexuality—not when the alternatives are vaguely defined and weighted down by metaphor and when the surrounding social group confounds reality with fantasy. In establishing a psychosexual identity, even the adolescent psychosocial moratorium provides few social supports, especially in societies like ours, in which sexuality is, in general, a source of anxiety and confusion.

In this chapter, we will consider how adolescents achieve adult sexual identities and a conception of themselves as masculine or feminine. We will begin by defining some key concepts and by considering how the individual's sexual and sex-role identity develops. We will look at the role of physical and cognitive development and socialization processes in this aspect of the identity-formation process. We also will consider how parent-child relationships, identifications, and peer-group interactions affect this development. Finally, we will look at the implications of psychosexual identity for psychological differences between the sexes.

Sexual and Sex-Role Identity

As part of the general adolescent identity-formation process, a psychosexual identity consisting of both a sexual identity and a sex-role identity is elaborated. The term *sexual identity* refers to that dimension of ego identity that reflects the adolescent's emerging ability to be a fully sexual being, capable of entering into intimate physical and emotional relationships with others. Younger children may have notions of parenthood, may engage in sexual play, and may have strong sexual curiosities; adolescents must integrate sexuality into their self-concept, must move toward participation in intimate sexual relations, must consider seriously the development of a long-term relationship with a member of the opposite sex, and must deal in some way, responsibly or otherwise, with the possibility of "making babies." The development of this sexual identity does not take place all at once but moves from early "puppy love" or aggressively exploratory types of relationships to more serious ones.

In addition to confronting issues relating to sexual functioning, adolescents begin, consciously and self-consciously, to question their sex-role identity: "How feminine (or masculine) am I?" Children display sex-typed behaviors, or behaviors that in a given society are more typical of one sex than the other, long before adolescence. However, a conscious and intense comparison of one's own sex-role characteristics with a cultural standard and a developing self-concept that incorporates a self-assessment of one's masculinity or femininity are more likely to characterize the adolescent years.

> I was a rather unattractive child until age 16, when I "blossomed" over a period of about a year. Teasing and ridicule accompanied me and culminated in the early teens when children seem to be most acutely aware of the changes within themselves and in the opposite sex, with special concern about their own appearance, and overly obsessed with sex in general. To be perfectly honest, concern about peer relationships and opposite sex relationships was predominant and most powerful all through the teen years. An unattractive appearance and insecurity about it made me dateless and full of anxiety and humiliation. An unfortunate overemphasis on one's social life existed in high school, and it seemed that I was not the only girl who anxiously awaited the days of togetherness with one of the opposite sex. Close and binding friendships with one or two girls was extremely important at this time. There were long notes, endless telephone calls and

study halls where men and sex were the major subjects of discussion. Looking back (of course from the security of previous and present relationships with men, now) I feel sad that I did not devote more time and interest in intellectual pursuits and academics.

The development of sexual identity and sex-role identity are interrelated and mutually dependent processes. An adequate sexual identity, providing a sense of self-esteem in presexual and sexual relationships, is important to sex-role identity. Eager to think of herself as a budding and feminine young woman, the early adolescent girl may rush into dating with older boys. Similarly, the pubescent boy who is unsure of his masculinity may engage in early heterosexual activities to strengthen his masculine self-concept (Kagan, 1964). At the same time, the endeavor of some young adolescents to be super-feminine or super-masculine in appearance and behavior may be part of an attempt to prepare and become desirable for future sexual relationships.

There is, on the other hand, no necessary and rigid relationship between sexual identity and sex-role identity—although people often confound sex-typed behavior with sexuality. Many people assume that all male ballet dancers are homosexual because they are engaging in a "feminine" activity. Yet many male dancers have both a firm heterosexual identity and a masculine self-concept. Moreover, there are big, strong, burly "hard hats" who have a homosexual identity and a concept of themselves in either a masculine or a feminine sex role.

Unfortunately, the general tendency to confound sex-typed behavior with sexuality has its impact on many a pubescent youngster. The boy who does not like aggressive sports but enjoys listening to classical music may begin, like some of the people around him, to see himself as less than masculine. He then may come to fear that he must be at least a latent homosexual, especially if strong taboos on heterosexuality have led him to any of the usual homosexual activities with peers. On the basis of clinical experience, Coons (1970) notes that many times parents fail to encourage their son's heterosexual development in high school because they are satisfied with his athletic or academic achievement. In college, these young men may confuse lack of heterosexual experience with homosexuality.

Development of Sexual and Sex-Role Identity

Psychosexual identity, like the more general process of identity formation, has its roots in earlier developmental stages. First to emerge is gender identity, or the child's self-categorization as a boy or a girl (Kohlberg,

1966). Gender identity is achieved only gradually, between the ages of 2 and 7, as the child masters gender constancy. That is, just as children of these ages learn to conserve amount and weight in Piagetian problems, they learn that one's sex stays the same regardless of clothing, length of hair, and other changes in appearance. (We know a 3-year-old girl who currently insists that she is going to be a "big boy" when she grows up. And a 5-year-old boy's refusal to put on a witch costume for Halloween reveals his lack of gender constancy, or his fear that putting on female outfits will make him a female.)

Gender identity generally, but not always, corresponds to one's biological sex. Transsexuals are those individuals who are convinced that their biologically assigned sex is inconsistent with their true gender identity—their inner feeling of maleness or femaleness (Fleming & Feinbloom, 1975). It is not unusual for a transsexual to complain of being a female trapped in a male body or a male trapped in a female body. Moreover, most transsexuals report having had feelings of being different from other people since they were 2 or 3 years old—that is, since the early years of gender-identity formation (Fleming & Feinbloom, 1975).

It is only after learning to identify themselves as girls or boys that children come to value girl or boy things and to want to behave in girl or boy ways (Kohlberg, 1966). Thus, sex-role identity follows gender identity. Once a child has learned, for example, to identify herself as a girl, she is anxious to conform to social expectations concerning what little girls do and do not do. Certainly everyone is ready to tell children—particularly boys—the "appropriate" way to behave. Children strive to display sex-typed behaviors not just because of rewards and punishments or because of desires to be like some powerful role model but also because of their own basic tendency toward cognitive consistency (Kohlberg, 1966).

That children may be rather sure of their gender identity and may be behaving in ways appropriate to their sex role by age 7 does not mean that their psychosexual identity is established. Puberty brings changes, often anticipated with anxiety as well as with excitement, that signal both to adolescents and to the adults around them that the capacity for adult sexuality is emerging. It is likely that almost all adolescents are concerned about the changes taking place in their bodies, fearing that the changes are taking place either too quickly or too slowly. It is quite possible that few adolescents feel in step with their peers in physical development and that most adolescents sometimes feel "freaky" because of the changes taking place. Besides the breasts that are suddenly too big or interminably too small, the penis and testes that refuse to enlarge, the body weight that is excessive or inadequate, and the Vesuvius-like eruptions on the face, there are also, suddenly, the nose that has become too large, the eyes that have become too small, and the hair that has become too straight or too curly.

The intense preoccupation of adolescents with their appearance is a product not only of physical changes but also of cognitive changes. As part of their logical development, adolescents grow in their ability to take the role of the other; they begin to see themselves as others see them. As is true at earlier stages of logical development, this emergence of more mature cognitive abilities is accompanied by an egocentrism of sorts.

At least two aspects of this cognitive egocentrism can be identified in many young adolescents; these are the imaginary audience and the personal fable (Elkind, 1967). With their new awareness that others can think about them just as they can think about others, many adolescents become convinced that others are thinking the same things about them that they are thinking about themselves. Elkind calls this phenomenon a preoccupation with an *imaginary audience*. Thus, the young girl may be sure that whatever aspect of her physique is most in her own thoughts is also in everyone else's thoughts. A boy may spend a whole evening thinking that his date is thinking about his pimples, while she spends the whole evening thinking that he is thinking about her fuzzy hair.

As part of their growing ability to consider the purely hypothetical, adolescents also may devote considerable time to spinning out great fantasies of which they, of course, are the heroines and heroes—and sometimes the victims. Frequently, but not always, these fantasies are focused on sex, and, as likely as not, they involve conquest and prowess for the boys, and love and romance for the girls.

> My life revolved around the fantasy that Paul McCartney was my brother (of all things). Maybe this was because I'm an only child. Actually, it was the most convenient relationship to have—I felt I was closer to him than any girlfriend could be, all the kids in school envied me for knowing him so well, everyone wanted to be friendly with me so they could meet him, I looked just like him, he cared for me more than anyone else, and I was also able to be friendly with the other three Beatles.

> One important thing was that no sex was involved in this relationship— I would be able to walk in on him when he wasn't dressed or when he was in the shower but I could never imagine any other type of sexual relationship with him or anyone else for that matter. I used to make my girlfriend draw me pictures of what her older brother looked like naked. She was a terrible artist.

Sexuality

While cognitive development provides the processes by which adolescents dream up a number of life scripts for themselves, the social environment contributes in important ways to the content of mental life. It seems likely that the preoccupation of North American adolescents with their bodies stems from the same motivation as the preoccupation of North American adults with youth and attractiveness—an obsession with sex and sexuality. In the United States, which has been one of the more sexually repressive countries of the world (Group for the Advancement of Psychiatry, 1971), sexuality has been struggling for some time to come "out of the closet." As a result, everyone is flooded with sexual stimuli. In all the media, sex is what sells. Still, this does not mean that sex is now considered good. Indeed, while anybody can go to the movies and view violence, which apparently is only natural and acceptable and rated G or PG, young people must be over 17 or be accompanied by an adult before they can view men and women engaging in intimate relationships in an R-rated movie. Anything as societally taboo as sex is likely to preempt a good deal of people's thinking.

While adolescents may share in some adult preoccupations, they are not adults. In our society, there are no initiation rites in which adults say to the adolescent, "Now you are a woman" or "Now you are a man." Nor does the arrival of puberty convey this message to young adolescents—not when they still have curfews, allowances, homework, restrictions, rules, and regulations. In our society, the achievement of puberty does not grant teen-agers adult social roles. They do not break away immediately from their own biological families, begin new families, take on their own financial support, or become participants in governing agencies. Nor can they immediately begin to engage in adult sexual roles. A long period of experimentation lies ahead before young people can gain full confidence in their own sexuality.

Puberty, however, undoubtedly intensifies the individual's concern with becoming an adult. Once a girl begins menstruating, motherhood is not just a dream or a distant possibility; it is a reality and even a danger. While heterosexuality becomes increasingly attractive and even, through social pressures, increasingly obligatory, the girl is warned against the evils of premature motherhood. That these warnings may be vague and not related clearly to any specific set of behaviors ("Don't do anything you shouldn't") only increases the girl's worry over what she should and should not do to be both a good girl and a young woman preparing for an adult role.

It is not the danger of pregnancy alone that can make the beginning of menstruation a problem as well as a milestone. Even girls who value "feminine" traits of warmth, nurturance, and sensitivity to others may feel ambivalent about becoming women in a society that devalues their sex. Many girls may anticipate a future in which they "can't win"—in which they see themselves as either facing drudgery and boredom as domestic slaves or being labeled "unfeminine" because they are competing in a "man's world." In the past, menstruation may have been a positive and welcomed signal to many girls that they were becoming women. Today, menstruation may only intensify concern with the question "What kind of woman will I be?"

First ejaculation may be for boys what first menstruation is for girls—a sign greeted with ambivalence as well as with satisfaction that sexual maturity is in the offing. The fact that ours is a male-oriented society in which men traditionally have been viewed as enjoying more freedom, sexual and otherwise, does not mean that manhood is faced without fear. How, after all, can a boy be sure that he truly is becoming a man and becoming one fast enough and adequately enough? A number of legal and social constraints prevent the youngster from attaining adult status by such means as obtaining a full-time job. For some, participation in delinquent activities may serve to confirm masculinity. For others, engaging in masturbatory, homosexual, or heterosexual activities may seem like the only way of proving to oneself and to others that one is a man; unfortunately, none of these methods is without costs. Sexual prowess takes practice, and there are few helpful guidelines available. Moreover, taboos learned early in life make all three modes of release—masturbation, homosexual behaviors, and heterosexual behaviors— sources of anxiety and guilt.

> Although my social contacts were limited in high school, I did attend a few parties. I was very nervous and unsure of myself, but I was determined to make headway with a girl. When the situation did develop, I was surprised at my success. I found a pretty blond who was very friendly. I forced myself to overcome my fear of rejection, and I asked her for a date. I can't remember ever being so happy as I was when she accepted. However, this happiness came to an abrupt end. I was totally unprepared for what was to come. The date turned into a complete disaster.

> I was preoccupied with how I should act and what I should say. I had an immense feeling of inadequacy that made me hyperanxious and miserable. The result was that during the date I didn't talk much. I felt I should be doing or saying something but could hardly say a thing. I felt terribly awkward and believed that the girl was disappointed in me. I was immensely disappointed with myself. The date was total misery and I was quite relieved when it was over. I didn't have another date for a long time.

Socialization Processes in Sex-Role Development

We have seen that the preoccupations and fears of the larger society contribute to adolescent concerns with sexuality. In addition, socialization pressures interact with physical and cognitive changes in the development of adolescent sex-role identity. Socialization forces tend to shape boys and girls to become different from each other and to provide the sex-role standards against which boys and girls compare themselves.

There is considerable, if not always consistent, evidence that, almost from birth, boys and girls are treated differently. Even before young children have established their gender identity, their gender seems to determine the kinds of responses they evoke from adults. For example, baby boys seem to be handled more roughly and treated as if they are less fragile than baby girls (Moss, 1967; Tasch, 1952; Yarrow, Rubenstein, & Pedersen, 1971). At least in well-educated families, mothers may vocalize more distinctly to girls than to boys (Kagan, 1971). Even the rooms of young boys and girls can reveal parental ideas about the appropriateness of different furnishings and different toys for each sex (Rheingold & Cook, 1975). Perhaps these early differences in treatment and interaction give rise to behavioral differences that lead people to think of boys as more "physical" and girls as more "verbal."

It is not only that boys and girls are treated differently and thereby reinforced for different behaviors, but also that they tend actively to *identify* with people of their own sex who serve as models of behavior. It has long been assumed that children learn their sex roles at least partially through identification with a parent. However, there is considerable theoretical controversy and empirical inconsistency in regard to such issues as how identification should be defined, which parent is more important to sex-role development, and whether identification is the only or even the principal mechanism in sex-role learning.

Johnson (1963), building on a theory first articulated by Parsons (1958), defines identification as the internalization of what she calls a reciprocal role relationship. In this view, identification can include any behavior that a child learns in interaction with a parent. These learned behaviors are not necessarily those performed, or modeled, by the parent but are perhaps the ones that the parent systematically evokes and reinforces in the child. Personality development, which includes sex-role development, takes place as a series of successive identifications with increasingly specialized and differentiated roles learned in interaction with parents and other role figures. Both boys and girls initially identify with the mother, since she is the primary caretaker. However, it is subsequent identification with the father that is crucial for both sexes. It is only the father, Johnson holds, who differentially reinforces behavior that is appropriate to the child's sex.

A rather different point of view is provided by Lynn (1966), who also builds on concepts articulated by Parsons (1958). Lynn agrees that, initially, both males and females identify with their mothers; in his view, however, this early maternal identification tends to continue to be of critical importance. In our society, he holds, parental identification is relatively easy for females, who generally have their mothers available as role models. However, because of full-time employment and other cultural variables, fathers are less available as models. Consequently, boys must rely on identification with a culturally defined male role, which is superimposed on an early identification with their mothers. Boys, then, are more anxious about their sex-role identities than are girls and are more likely to incorporate characteristics of the opposite sex in their sex-role identities.

We believe that there is some truth to both Johnson's and Lynn's views (see Gray & Klaus, 1956; Heilbrun, 1965). We also believe that each view is incomplete and somewhat oversimplified. There is no overwhelming evidence to support Johnson's notion that fathers, but not mothers, are capable of interacting in both expressive and instrumental roles. Nor is there overwhelming evidence to support Lynn's notion that fathers are unavailable as role models. It seems likely that in the average family boys and girls internalize characteristics of both parents, that both parents serve as role models at least some of the time, and that both tend to reinforce different behaviors in their sons and daughters.

There is more to the development of sex roles than this, however. One of the major shortcomings of Johnson's and Lynn's approaches is the basic assumption that becoming "feminine" or "masculine" depends rather exclusively on identification. While Johnson stretches the term "identification" to include behaviors acquired through reinforcement, a more complete approach to determining the causes of sex-role development is needed. This involves distinguishing among identification as defined in the Freudian tradition (the internalization of parental values), socialization (the internalization of social norms and values), and other processes. The findings of one study making these distinctions (Block, Von der Lippe, & Block, 1973) will be examined in some detail.

In this study, men and women are divided into four groups on the basis of whether they score high or low in their adherence to sex-typed values and whether they score high or low in their adherence to more general social values. Four different patterns of familial antecedents can be identified. Individuals who score high in the endorsement of both sex-typed behaviors and normative social values reveal a pattern of "identification with the same-sex parent in a context of familial harmony and traditional parental role definitions" (Block, Von der Lippe, & Block, 1973, p. 335). Individuals who score low in traditional sex typing but high in socialization show a pattern of "androgynous identification,"[1] or "the modeling of a parental pair in which neither father nor mother exemplify the typical cultural sex role stereotypes but rather where both parents provide models for their children of competence, tolerance, consideration of others and sharing of responsibilities" (p. 336).

___

[1] *Androgyny* refers to the combination of both "masculine" and "feminine" characteristics, or expressive and instrumental behaviors in a single personality. We will be discussing this type of psychosexual identity more fully in the final section of this chapter.

These two patterns of identification are contrasted (Block, Von der Lippe, & Block, 1973) with "reactivity" and "counteractivity." Reactive individuals are high in sex-role typing but low in socialization and seem to come from families in which the same-sex parent is neurotic and rejecting. Sex-role typing is achieved reactively through reinforcement by the opposite-sex parent. Finally, there are men and women who are low in both sex-role typing and socialization. Those counteractive individuals, coming from families characterized by conflict and psychopathology, seem to acquire their sex-role definitions and value orientations through a counteractive process. That is, they deliberately define themselves as different from an emotionally detached same-sex parent and emulate the characteristics of the opposite-sex parent.

These distinctions between sex-role typing and socialization seem helpful, as do the distinctions among identification, reactivity, and counteractivity. The search for antecedents of different patterns of sex-role identity and socialization values also is useful. However, we believe that even this view of sex-role development is incomplete. What is lacking in the approaches of Johnson (1963), Lynn (1966), and J. Block et al. (1973)—and indeed in most theories of psychosexual development that emphasize the role of socializing forces—is an adequate account of the developing child and the individual characteristics that the child brings to any socializing encounter. We will return to the elaboration of a developmental model after examining the role of socializing forces beyond the family.

Further Socialization

After establishing gender identities, boys and girls gradually move into broader social spheres, which also contribute to their differential socialization. Nursery-school teachers (Serbin, O'Leary, Kent, & Tonick, 1973), like parents, are more harsh in their disciplining of boys than of girls. There seems to be little doubt that boys receive more physical punishment than girls (Maccoby & Jacklin, 1974). Since it does not seem to be true that boys are reinforced for aggression more than girls are (Maccoby & Jacklin, 1974), it may be that any tendency for little boys to behave more aggressively than little girls (Serbin et al., 1973) is a result of their modeling themselves on the behaviors of adults.

As a result of both socialization pressures and their own cognitive tendency to behave in ways that are consistent with their self-definition, boys and girls increasingly diverge into two fundamentally different orientations: the instrumental versus the expressive, or the agentic versus the communal (Bakan, 1966; Carlson, 1971; Parsons, 1958). The stereotype of the male that persists in our society portrays him as an instrumental fighter of battles and protector of women and children—a goal-directed, autonomous, rational being. His relationships are agentic, or means to ends rather than ends in themselves. The stereotype of the female, in contrast, portrays her as an expressive caretaker—empathic, nurturing, and emotional. Her relationships are communal; they are ends in themselves. It is from caring and from interpersonal relationships that her life derives its meaning.

As adults, we may want to say "But these portraits *are* stereotypes. They don't apply to all men and women, and if they were ever true at all they're becoming less and less true." However, there is no evidence that children view these stereotypes as anything less than realities. From an early age, children report that fathers are bigger and stronger, more powerful, more fearless, and smarter than mothers. Fathers are described as both the ones who work and the ones who control the family (Kagan, 1964; Kohlberg, 1966). Fathers also are seen as less loving, less friendly, stricter, and more prone to using physical punishment (Becker, 1964). These opinions seem to be held rather widely by children, regardless of who does the disciplining in their family and how, or whether or not their own mother works. Given their limitations of cognitive development, children seem unable to differentiate between myth and reality and unable to integrate information that is discrepant with a blatant cultural stereotype.

Does all this change with the advent of adolescence? Quite the contrary. Pubescent youngsters may be the most desperate conformers of all. Young adolescents (13 to 14) are more likely than older adolescents (18 to 21) to conform to peer judgments in a number of psychological tasks (Costanzo & Shaw, 1966; Landsbaum & Willis, 1971). This tendency to conform may be particularly relevant to sexual-identity development when young adolescents are going through what Erikson (1968) calls a period of bisexual confusion. This confusion is characterized by adolescents' obsessive preoccupation with the question of what kind of man or woman, or deviate, they may become. Without understanding how much leeway can be encompassed in femininity or masculinity, young adolescents may choose the most conservative path, adhering strictly to the cultural stereotype. As Erikson puts it, these adolescents may fear that to be a little less of their own sex is to be all of the other.

The expression of a heightened concern with masculinity and femininity may be found, surprisingly enough, in data on delinquency. About three-quarters of all delinquents are boys, and three-quarters of these are in the early-adolescent age range of 14 to 16 years (Hauck, 1970). That theft is a major form of delinquent activity may indicate that such characteristics of the male role as courage, daring, and autonomy have been misconstrued to mean a flaunting of authority. Delinquent acts are not confined to lower-class youth. In one study, more than 70% of the upper-class and 64% of the middle-class boys admitted to participating in petty theft (Vaz, 1969).

Consistent with their greater conformity to rules, adolescent girls are less likely than boys to engage in delinquent activities. However, the stress felt by some girls is reflected in relatively high anxiety and personal adjustment problems. When young adolescent girls *are* delinquent, the female sex-role stereotype is maintained in the nature of their delinquency (Hauck, 1970).

The development of sexual activities also shows the impact of cultural stereotypes. In North America, males are supposed to be the aggressors, and females are supposed to be the resisters. These patterns tend to characterize heterosexual interactions right from the beginning of dating. The impact of cultural stereotypes goes even deeper than this. The boy's sexual behavior continues the traditional masculine concern with competition, achievement, success, and using relationships as means to ends. Locker-room talk does not limit itself to discussions of who is the best batter and who has the longest throwing arm; nor is discussion of what base one can get to confined to the topic of baseball.

The cultural characteristic of competitiveness has some relevance for girls as well as for boys in Western society. While male success in competition may be defined in terms of "how far you can go," female success may be measured by the number of boys who are flocking after you, as long as the boys' attentions are not attracted by your "looseness."

While competition among girls is socially acceptable, competition of girls with boys is unacceptable after puberty. Where is the teenager who doesn't know that boys are supposed to beat girls at swimming, at tennis, at being elected class president—at almost everything? Throughout elementary school, girls surpass boys in academics. After junior high school, this picture is generally reversed. Those girls who continue to do better than boys academically may go to great lengths to conceal that fact.

> The years 11 to 14 were a much more difficult period than the preceding ones. I was happy in elementary school. I was in the "smart class" and I was chosen to represent the school on a T.V. quiz show. This was okay when you are in elementary school—but once you got to junior high, forget it! You weren't *supposed* to be too smart—I ended up dropping two of my honor classes—I didn't want to be one of those "smartees"!!!

Even in high school, there are courses in which the superior performance of girls is acknowledged. Almost everybody knows that girls are supposed to do better in English and boys in mathematics and science. However, many girls actually do very well in mathematics and science (but probably quietly and frequently with great secrecy). How is it, then, that in adulthood there are so few women who reach eminence in these areas? It may be that being secretly good in science, which is helpful to high school girls, works against their later success in that field. In a study of over 2000 students enrolled in Harvard's extensive Project Physics, Walberg (1969) found that girls outscored boys on measures of verbal aptitude, docility, dependency, and willingness to work. All of these characteristics may contribute to success in science at the high school level but detract from later success. Walberg postulates a discontinuity between feminine and scientific roles as part of the explanation for the relative paucity of females reaching eminence in science.

One might assume that by late adolescence individuals are secure enough in their sexual identities, as well as mature enough in their cognitive development, to loosen up in their conformity to sex-role stereotypes. While this pattern of increasing flexibility may be true of many adolescents, it is by no means a universal pattern. Modern-day college students not only describe the "average" man and woman in ways that are highly consistent with cultural stereotypes, but they also describe themselves, and even their ideal selves, in ways consistent with the stereotypes. College women report that they are, in reality and ideally, more emotional, more dependent, less rational, and less autonomous than men (Broverman et al., 1972).

Sexual Knowledge (and Miseducation)

While adolescents may be rigid in their interpretation of femininity and masculinity, they at least know clearly and with overwhelming consensus what the cultural stereotypes are. Their knowledge of sex-role stereotypes, however, is not matched by a knowledge of human sexuality. Both male and female college students overestimate the extent of their sex knowledge in some areas. Some males greatly overestimate their understanding of sexual structure and function and venereal disease, while their female peers overestimate their understanding of venereal disease, conception, and masturbation (McCreary-Juhasz, 1967). While there are individual and group differences in how much is known on any given sexual topic, there may be no topic on which everyone is well-informed. The tremendous expansion of telephone sex-information services testifies to the public's growing awareness of its misinformation and lack of information in sexual matters.

Given the abysmal state of sex education, sexual ignorance among adolescents, and even adults, should not be regarded as surprising. As Payne (1970) points out, children learn all kinds of fables when they're small; however, while deceptions about Santa Claus and the Easter bunny get revised, those concerning sex may never be dealt with directly. Many parents make no attempt to initiate sex education once their children reach puberty, regardless of whether or not they have made any attempts to do so earlier (Schofield, 1965, reported in Payne, 1970).

Cultural taboos about sexuality, combined with the impoverished level of sex education, can only exacerbate sex-related problems. Ignorance about birth control combined with a knowledge of the stereotyped "good girl" has never served to reduce the rate of unmarried pregnancies. In one study (Wagner, 1970), pregnant teenagers were asked why they had not used contraceptives. The answer, of course, was "I am not that kind of girl." The use of contraceptives is an indication of "premeditated sex," which is a double evil—sex outside of marriage and in cold blood (Wagner, 1970).

It should be clear that the increasing sexual intimacy that characterizes adolescent heterosexual relationships is not just a matter of postpubertal lust or of some animalistic sexual drive. It is part of the process by which adolescents, often with very little help from adults, prepare for adult roles as procreators and parents. It is also part of the process by which adolescents learn about themselves as sexual beings and as individuals becoming mature enough to begin really caring for others and not just being taken care of by others.

> Men were very important to me. It was on this field I fought my hardest battles, partially because I defined myself in terms of men. I still define myself in this way and am not quite sure it is a healthy way to live. I have always had a boyfriend and would probably feel lost without one.
> Drugs and politics never affected me. They were just not a part of the world I had carved out for myself. Sex, on the other hand, consumed me. Knowing, of course, it wasn't for "nice" girls like me but being so terribly curious. And once when a girl got pregnant being just a tiny bit envious because after all she *knew*.

Adolescent Relationships

While there are countless paths by which adolescents can attain heterosexual maturity and a secure sex-role self-concept, Feinstein and Ardon (1973) have identified what may be a general pattern of development. First is the phase of "sexual awakening"; both sexes, at approximately 13 to 15 years of age, become aware of their developing sexual potential. Boys at this age may feel some psychological insecurity in their relationships with girls because the girls reach physical maturity before they do. (Remember those dances in junior high school when many of the girls were taller than the boys?) During this phase, there may be the most rigid adherence to sex-typed behavior, along with considerable reliance on same-sex peers for the definition of appropriate behavior.

Second is the phase, at ages 14 to 17, of "practicing," characterized by numerous short-term relationships with the opposite sex and by irregular dating. Boys and girls in this phase go beyond same-sex relationships. Experimentation with the opposite sex strengthens sex role and sexual identities. It is not sex alone, then, but also role experimentation that is the guiding motivation of these early interactions.

The phase of "practicing" is followed by a gradual acceptance of a sex role and a sexual identity at about 16 to 19 years of age. During this phase, adolescents master the basic aspects of a sexual relationship and generally achieve increasing comfort in heterosexual relationships. Finally, between the ages of 18 and 25, and even later, comes the development of, in Freudian terms, a "permanent object choice," or a relatively stable choice of a partner for a long-term relationship. By this time, many adolescents have achieved enough security in their identity formation to be capable of true intimacy, not just a physical relationship with another.

This pattern of development corresponds rather well with what we know about the development of adolescent social relationships (Dunphy, 1963). Early adolescents, confronted with new social expectations at puberty, shift their dependency needs from the family to small unisexual cliques. These cliques are, or become, subsystems in "crowds," which are, in turn, composed of both all-male and all-female cliques and of more mature, heterosexual cliques.

During middle adolescence, these unisexual cliques begin to break down (Dunphy, 1963). Gradually, as individuals establish significant relationships with members of the opposite sex, a new clique system evolves and groups become heterosexual. The "crowd" as a social system seems to persist long enough to help individuals achieve security in their new roles and evolving identities and then breaks up as couples establish more enduring relationships. Dunphy (1963) interprets the role of the peer group in this process as an extension of socialization within the family, with a similar differentiation along instrumental and expressive lines.

The Peer Group

The development of the individual's sex role and sex-role identity during adolescence undoubtedly depends a good deal on interactions with both same-sex and opposite-sex peers. Indeed, the peer group seems to have considerable importance in setting the norms for acceptable sexual and sex-role behavior. For example, sexually aggressive college males who admit to "pushing girls further than they want to go despite crying and serious protests" report having friends who advocate an active sex life (Kanin, 1967), In fact, the young men who report same-sex peer pressure to participate in sexual encounters also report sexual dissatisfaction—even though they may be engaging in considerably more sexual activity than are less sexually aggressive individuals. Sexual frustration almost seems to follow from, rather than lead to, sexual aggression, perhaps because no sexual experience, and especially not a "forced" experience, can match the expectations that are set by the peer group.

The characteristics that define a peer group are complex. For example, you may know a number of people who are the same age as you but who are not, psychologically, your peers. (Some people you listen to, and some you don't.) A number of studies have attempted to identify the broad social influences, both within the family and within the peer group, that influence sexual attitudes and behaviors. These studies have run aground when examining only such gross variables as social class. There seems to be no strong relationship between social class and either early (before age 18) intercourse (Simon, Berger, & Gagnon, 1972) or permissive sexual attitudes (Reiss, 1965). There is a stronger relationship between dating frequency, which varies considerably among peer groups, and amount of sexual experience (Simon, Berger, & Gagnon, 1972). There is also a strong relationship between one's liberal or conservative background, as defined by locale, religious status, marital status, political views, and so on, and one's attitudes toward sex (Reiss, 1965).

> The social pressure was enormous. I remember feeling that I should go out with girls in junior high school not so much because I wanted to but because it was the thing to do . . . the thing to do if you were cool. There was also social pressure to have the right friends. Certain people were the people you should be with and other students were social outcasts. It was clear where one stood by your contact with other students. I spent a great deal of my time daydreaming and fantasizing and escaping into sports to avoid feeling my unhappiness.

Ethnic group also seems to be a more powerful predictor of sexual behavior and attitudes than is social class. Rosenberg & Bensman (1968) examined sexual mores in three ethnic subcultures, each a transmigrated group living in poverty: white Appalachians living in Chicago, Southern Blacks living in Washington, D.C., and Puerto Ricans living in New York City. These three groups differed sharply from one another in regard to patterns of sexual behavior. The only common factor was their treatment of females as necessary but unequal partners. All three groups differed from the North American middle class in sexual behavior but differed no more strongly than they did from one another.

Groups differ not only in their sexual attitudes and behavior but also in how consistent their attitudes are with their behaviors. Reiss (1968) reports on a study, done by Christensen and Carpenter in 1962, of Danish, Midwestern, and Utah college students. This study found that the Danish students had the most permissive sexual attitudes but were most likely not to have done as much as they believed permissible. The Utah students, by contrast, had the least permissive attitudes but were most likely to have done more than they believed was proper.

Socialization forces stemming from the family, the peer group, and the broader society have a role in psychosexual development, but they are not the final determinants of psychosexual identity. Conformity to norms is not the highest achievement in moral development nor is it the highest achievement in psychosexual development. Where adolescence is prolonged and alternatives are available, development carries the individual beyond conformity. It is to a developmental perspective that we now return.

Toward Androgyny

We have noted that, as part of their identity development, adolescents must deal with issues relating to their psychosexual identities. We also have seen that adolescents have new cognitive structures that allow them to consider alternative selves and to reflect on the directions in which they are moving. We also remarked at the beginning of this chapter that advanced cognitive structures provide no guarantee of any easy solution to complicated and emotionally charged problems.

In psychosexual development, as in moral-judgment development, there seems to be a delay in the adolescent's ability to deal with issues at the level of his or her "best thinking." Even though many of them have begun to achieve the highest stage of cognitive development, high school students generally do not move beyond Stage 4 in moral judgment; that is, they maintain the status-quo morality. Even after a year or two of college, many students are functioning at Stage 4½ thinking and are not yet able to resolve the contradictions involved in rejecting conventional morals while insisting that acts *can* be judged for their rightness or goodness. Not until well into the college years or beyond are there some individuals capable of reasoning with a higher-law, or a conscience, orientation.

A powerful case can be made for the argument that adolescents' judgments concerning sexual and sex-role behavior are very much dependent upon their overall stage of moral development (see Pleck, 1975). If this argument is correct, one would expect high school students typically to uphold strict conformity to sexual and sex-role norms. Whatever their own behavior, adolescents frequently do seem to insist loudly on adherence to codes. Thus, the young adolescent boy who persuasively, aggressively, and determinedly deflowers a girl turns around to disparage her failure to be a "good girl." And regardless of what other girls are doing, they too will disparage the "bad girl." Moreover, it probably is not only anxiety about their own sexuality but also a form of Stage 4 moral judgment that leads gangs of middle or late adolescent boys into the city to seek out and beat up "queers."

Fortunately, this rigid sexual morality does not seem to be the end point of psychosexual identity development. Just as some people move toward a postconventional morality that requires the exercise of individual conscience, some people move toward a psychological androgyny, which requires flexibility and tolerance in the definition of what is appropriate in sexual and sex-role behavior. Individuals who achieve an androgynous sexual identity are able to combine the masculine and the feminine, the instrumental and the expressive, and the agentic and the communal in their own functioning. Does this result in effeminate men and mannish women? No, it appears to result in individuals who have a much broader range of adaptive behavior in many situations than do peers who act only in stereotyped ways. For example, Bem (1975) found that androgynous college students of both sexes were able to display both independence when under pressure to conform and playfulness when given a chance to play with a kitten—although each of these activities had been independently rated as "more typical" of one sex than the other. In contrast, more traditionally sex-typed students, especially the feminine females, were found to display a range of behavioral deficits. There is also evidence that androgynous individuals receive more honors and awards, date more, and have a lower incidence of childhood illness (Spence, Helmreich, & Stapp, 1975).

One's personal value system and one's psychosexual identity are mutually important components of ego identity. It is interesting that in these most vital and personal areas, individuals generally are unable to think as flexibly and with as much sophistication as they are able to when they are dealing with physical problems "out there" in the world. Philosophers, social critics, and psychologists long have noted that mankind's intellect seems to have outstripped its ethical and emotional growth. A lag between cognitive and ethical development seems to characterize individual development as well as social development.

In the concluding chapter, we will try briefly to put the individual back together—to look at cognitive, personality, moral-judgment, and psychosexual-identity development as they interrelate with one another. We will conclude with a final statement about adolescence as a stage and about the functions it serves for both the individual and society.

Chapter Seven

Adolescence in Context

Again, we ask "What is adolescence?" In some ways, it is a second chance. It is built upon the developments of childhood, but it opens up the possibility of new pathways to and through adulthood. After extending the syntheses begun in Chapter Two, we will consider how the achievements of the adolescent period influence adult development, the development of society, and the future of humanity.

Synthesis

In Chapter Two we presented an integrated view of cognitive and ego-identity development from infancy through adolescence. In this chapter, we would like to extend that perspective to include adolescents' major achievements in moral and psychosexual development.

During adolescence, many young people develop what Piaget calls formal-operational thinking. This level of cognitive development entails the capacity for Stage 3 moral judgments, or judgments oriented toward mutuality in interpersonal relations (Kohlberg, 1973) and a conscious concern with identity, including the question "What kind of woman or man will I become?" Whatever the behavior of young adolescents is, their moral judgments at this stage are conservative and nonautonomous. Rather than formulate their own moral codes, these young people incorporate the pre-digested codes of others. Herein lies part of the dilemma of many young adolescents. They are beginning to feel the need to achieve some separateness from their parents. They are subject to growing sexual awareness as well as to peer pressure to gain sexual experience. At the same time, their own moral reasoning, if not their behavior, expresses the assumption that morality requires people to be good and nice. Essentially, pubescent youngsters rely on their parents' values in judging abstract moral dilemmas, even though, on the concrete level, these values frequently include prohibitions against sexual activity. What often results is that teenagers assert their independence and experiment sexually but still feel that what they are doing is "dirty" or "bad" or in some manner wrong. (Remember those pregnant teenagers who wouldn't use contraceptives because they weren't "that kind of girl"?)

It long has been an assumption in adolescent psychology that teenagers turn to their peer group for emotional support. What has not always been recognized is the extent to which the early-adolescent peer group, like its individual members, is developmentally conservative in values. Brittain's findings (1963) that young adolescents tend to rely on peer-group judgments in superficial matters such as clothing styles and hair length but still rely on parental judgments in matters such as life plans and choice of potential mates are not surprising when viewed from a cognitive-developmental perspective.

With continued cognitive growth, adolescents become capable of moral judgments and value orientations that extend beyond the influence of the family to the influence of broader social groups. This is a characteristic of Stage 4 thinking. Still conservative in their judgment of abstract moral dilemmas, these individuals also praise solutions that contribute to the maintenance of the social order, of fixed rules, and of established authority. How, then, will these teenagers evaluate sexual behavior and sex-role stereotypes? To the extent that society in general frowns on sexual activities and deviation from sex-role stereotypes, so too will the Stage 4 youth. To the extent that society itself is ambivalent about these issues, the adolescent's judgments, too, will be beset with confusion and doubt. Given the sexual hang-ups of our society, much of the "crisis" of middle adolescence may reflect the attempt of young people to integrate into their identities a sexuality about which they feel considerable ambivalence. Moreover, as adolescents become aware that many adults only pay lip service to the sexual codes that they promulgate so loudly, anxiety concerning sexual mores can only increase.

The relationship between sexual behavior and self-esteem or mental health makes much more sense if it is viewed in light of a cognitive-developmental perspective. If some "promiscuous" college girls feel guilty about their sexual behavior to the point of extreme "alienation" (Halleck, 1967), it may be precisely because, whatever the reasons for their behavior, they basically accept the values of a society that condemns their behavior. The occurrence of guilt does not prove that promiscuous sexual behavior is unhealthy for the individual or for society; rather, it indicates that how a person feels about what she or he does is linked at least partly to cognitive maturity.

By late adolescence, many young people have achieved a level of cognitive development that permits a true identity crisis—not just a conflict with parents over clothes, hair length, or curfews and not just an internal conflict over what is right or wrong in heterosexual relationships—on a conscious level, a real questioning of themselves, their values, their society, and their goals. It seems likely that the moral reasoning of these youths has advanced enough to reflect a discomfort with conventional values but not enough to provide for a well-articulated postconventional system of reasoning. As part of their rejection of values that have a worth based only on convention, these young people would be likely to renounce both the sexual double standard and rigid conformity to sex-role stereotypes. Even in the midst of a psychosocial moratorium, however, such youths still might feel considerable doubt and anxiety about their psychosexual identities.

For those late adolescents or young adults whose cognitive development and experiences eventually provide a basis for postconventional moral judgment, an androgynous sexual identity that includes equality in sexual relations should become possible. Identity crises are not always resolved in the direction of an androgynous identity, but this resolution appears to be increasingly frequent. The traditional notions of "masculinity" as a distinguishing characteristic of the psychologically healthy man and "femininity" as a characteristic of the psychologically healthy woman are being questioned more and more (Bem, 1974; Block, 1973; Gump, 1972; Josselyn, 1970; Pleck, 1975). Androgynous individuals, in whom tenderness and autonomy can coexist peacefully, may be the best equipped to deal with the complex situations of today's, and tomorrow's, world.

The tragedy is, of course, that not everybody reaches their potential. Many people admit that they don't make maximum use of their intellectual capabilities—they don't need to. But if few people actualize their intellectual capabilities, even fewer achieve the level of moral judgment and the flexibility of psychosexual identity of which they are cognitively capable.

Adolescence and Beyond

If modern youth do not experience a crisis of identity and values, then the world is, indeed, in serious crisis. If everyone on this planet subscribes to the explicit convention that "Might makes right" and if the leaders of every country continue to view economics, politics, history, and, yes, ethics only from their own point of view, then we are indeed in trouble. As Erikson puts it, the tendency of individuals to identify themselves with "pseudospecies," or with national or ethnic identities, instead of with the human species, may spell the end for the human species.

What is adolescence? It is a psychosocial moratorium, a prolonged transition period between childhood and adulthood, which may or may not be embraced by the individual as an opportunity for soul-searching and for growth. The existence of adolescence as a social and developmental phenomenon has been described as an invention that meets at least two interrelated needs of a technocratic society: the need for extensive training of many youth for specialized occupations and the need to keep youth from competing on a job market in which there is less than ample employment. Its impact as a social and developmental phenomenon stems from the human potential to develop cognitive structures that raise the level of thought and that allow humans to transcend the bounds of their immediate and personal experience. Most significantly, these structures can lead to the development of ethical systems such as those of Christ or Gandhi and to an identity that allows one to understand all humanity—to walk in the shoes of another, to see the world through that other's eyes.

What does society gain by allowing—and imposing—this extended adolescence? It gains many young people who undergo a set of experiences and are faced with sets of problems that cannot be solved with concrete, unreflective, and time-worn solutions. It gains many young people who have had a chance to ask themselves who they are, how they got to be who they are, where they are going with their lives, and what they want to become. It gains individuals who recognize that laws are not always just and that justice is not always served by those who administer the laws—individuals who can be egalitarian in their dealings with race, sex, and ethnicity. Finally, an adolescent period provides a mechanism for change—a vital need in complex technical societies. Modern society changes constantly, if not always progressively. The adolescent who seeks, questions, and in part rejects the existing order serves as a human institution for change.

Depending on the time and the place, adolescence can be either an ending or a beginning. In the relatively unchanging, so-called primitive, societies, in which the same institutions, values, and practices are carried on *in perpetu,* adolescence is more of an ending than a beginning. In constantly changing, so-called advanced, societies, in which institutions and practices evolve and change, adolescence is more of a beginning than an ending; it is the period of time when the potential for the greatest adult achievements emerges. Margaret Mead (1949) states this well.

> One of the particular characteristics of a changing society is the possibility of deferred maturity, of later and later shifts in the lives of the most complex, the most flexible individuals. In very simple societies, children have completed their acceptance of themselves and their roles in life by the time they are six or seven, and then must simply wait for physical maturity to assume a complete role. But in most societies, adolescence is a period of re-examination, and possible re-orientation of the self toward the expressed

goals of society. In cultures like ours, there may be a second or a third adolescence, and the most complex, the most sensitive, may die still questing, still capable of change, starting like Franz Boas at 77 to reread the folklore of the world in the light of new theoretical developments [pp. 360-361].*

Many adults, like Gauguin, may reach a profound state of discomfort with their lives or with the world around them and may seek a "moratorium." The possibility of an adult experiencing a psychosocial crisis (and we do not see any need to attach the term *adolescent* to the productive, if sometimes distressful, self-examinations of adulthood) may be made more likely by his or her having experienced a crisis in adolescence. That is, once individuals open themselves up to an examination of themselves and their values, they may be more likely to open themselves up to such reexaminations again in the future. Certainly, self and social evaluation do not seem to be just age-linked phenomena undertaken by a few rebels in their youth and then abandoned forevermore. Differences in political ideology and behavior, for instance, persist well into adulthood.

In Piaget's theory, it is assumed that the highest level of cognitive development becomes achievable during adolescence. There are no further fundamental changes in actual cognitive ability if this adolescent potential is achieved. Erikson suggests that developmental change continues to occur after adolescence when individuals, now integrated in some way into their societies, meet additional psychosocial crises peculiar to young adulthood (intimacy versus isolation), the middle years (generativity versus stagnation), and old age (integrity versus despair).

In Erikson's view, the degree to which the crisis of young adulthood will be resolved successfully is highly dependent on the outcome of the adolescent identity crisis. The young adult must risk the identity that has been gained. That is, the young adult typically must face the required intimacies and demands of sexual union, marriage, potential offspring, and career. If identity has been achieved and identity diffusion has receded, then one is able to fuse one's identity with those of others—husband, wife, children, close friends—without fear of permanent ego loss. The danger of these years lies in the possibility of remaining isolated even within the context of family, friends, and career. Individuals with weak and diffuse identities may feel it necessary to protect themselves against what are seen as intrusions into, and a potential loss of, those identities. Such individuals may distance themselves from and even combat those who come too close.

What of the middle years? Under the best of circumstances, a family or other stable intimate relationship is established, a career or occupation is

*From *Male and Female,* by Margaret Mead. Copyright © 1949 by William Morrow and Company, Inc. Reprinted by permission.

well under way, and one is creative and productive in the manner for which talent and circumstance best provide. Does one reach another stage—still another psychosocial crisis of development? Erikson (1963), of course, says yes, the developmental process continues. In the middle adult years, the crisis seems to occur around the interdependence of the generations. Erikson's term *generativity* reflects not merely successful creation of new life or contribution to others but also refers to the personal gains that stem from caring for and guiding the next generation. Another outcome of the crisis of middle years may be *stagnation*. This stagnation often is reflected in depression—the loss of faith in self-worth—and in the kind of pseudo-intimacy with others that suggests loss of faith in one's family, society, and culture.

The crisis of old age is reflected in the polarity of ego integrity versus despair. In old age, one is no longer sustained by a full participation with members of all generations. That enriching source now has been given over. One may have, however, the sense of integrity that comes from knowing that there has been meaning in one's own style of having negotiated the prior stages of life. One can have a sense of order and of value in life. Despair reflects the sense that time is now too short and one cannot go back and repair or redo. Like intimacy and generativity, integrity demands a well-developed identity, giving individuals some sense of sureness and rightness about their roles, relationships, and accomplishments.

Conclusions

We have no idealistic view that adolescents now are better and brighter than those who went before them. Nor are we Rousseauians, believing that everybody would grow up just fine if only society would let them alone. We are impressed not so much by what is achieved during adolescence as by the potential—often neglected or rejected—for further growth and development that is made possible simply by the existence of an adolescent period. While many adolescents are very bright, we do not believe that they are overly endowed with wisdom. Wisdom demands a wealth of experience—adult, reflective, consciousness-raising, and responsible experience. Even under the best of circumstances, this accumulation of experience is only beginning in adolescence. And, unfortunately, neither intellectual potential nor any well-identified set of experiences ensures wisdom. Society is full of highly intelligent but bigoted maintainers of pseudospecies.

Observers of the human condition frequently have noticed that intellectual growth—particularly its expression in technology—has exceeded emotional and ethical development. It does seem that the most advanced forms of cognitive structure are necessary, but not sufficient, for the development of the most conscientious moral perspectives. It even seems that some sort of identity crisis and autonomous identity achievement—freeing us from the previously successful, but no longer adaptive, mores of many of our foreparents—is necessary, but not sufficient, for a fully conscientious and universal moral perspective. The greatest work in such cognitive areas as mathematical and pure physical theory has been undertaken during the late adolescence of the thinkers involved, but the major ethical ideologies have been formulated by much more mature individuals (Kohlberg, 1973). Moreover, the number of individuals showing achievement in mathematics and science may be far greater than the number showing an autonomously achieved identity and an ethical philosophy. We know something about the kinds of environments and experiences that help stimulate the development of what Piaget calls formal operations. But we know very little about the kinds of experiences that promote the achievement of an autonomous ego identity and the actualization of postconventional moral judgment. Certainly, higher education often seems to play some role in the broadening of human awareness, the presentation of alternative life styles and choices, and the stimulation of human achievements. Kohlberg (1973) reports in his longitudinal study of moral development that, while none of the subjects who went from high school immediately into the army or into adult occupations developed principled thinking, many of the subjects who went to college did. Rebelsky and Speisman (1975) have argued the importance of a liberal arts education, as opposed to a premature professionalism, in promoting maximum cognitive and moral development as well as in encouraging identity achievement.

Of course, education per se does not guarantee advanced ethical thinking, as demonstrated amply both by Hitler's Germany and by some of the well-educated jingoists and psychopaths of our own time. Nor should we assume that all young people should go immediately into college after high school. It is well known that one of the most exciting periods in American education occurred right after World War II, when college campuses were flooded with returning war veterans. Many of today's best thinkers—ethically as well as intellectually—came from this group of individuals, whose careers not only were interrupted by the war but also were turned in new directions.

Perhaps even more important than education, as it is traditionally defined, is experience that is truly *experienced*—experience that is truly personal and frequently emotional (Kohlberg, 1973). Such experience does not come out of books and does not engage just the mind. It is experience that is lived and not merely lived through. Particularly important, Kohlberg believes (1973), is the experience of sustained responsibility for the welfare of others—the same kind of experience that Erikson identifies as central to the achievement of human generativity.

We can only conclude that adolescence is a beginning that contains a promise—a promise that, unfortunately, is frequently not realized or is realized only in part. If we are to achieve a world peopled by individuals who are not only bright and educated but are also humane, we must first identify the experiences that contribute to the actualization of our highest potential.

Despite the popularity of the notion of "alienation" in the media, we believe that most young people are not so alienated by society that they have abandoned the hope of reforming it. Most of our students seem to look forward with optimism to their future and their role in society. Where identity achievement is accompanied by the achievement of a principled ethic, this optimism contains a real promise for society.

> As an adolescent, I was primarily concerned with intelligence over emotions. I have learned to deal much more effectively with feelings lately—both mine and others'—and this is important to me. Being sensitive to others' needs is crucial if understanding is ever to take place. I have learned to communicate on many different levels and I'm happier for it.
>
> Most of the confusion of adolescent years has worn off, and I think that the problems I am now facing are more "adult-like" in nature. Yet these new issues are a reflection of my past, and my future dreams and the troubled years of adolescence are still close to me. I no longer feel plagued by identity crisis, trouble with family relationships or peers, or morality problems. I feel that development is an ongoing process and growth is ever-present—but not as erratic these days. Because of this I think that adolescence does end—eventually—but it certainly has no definite age limit. I guess when the turmoil slows down and we feel more secure and confident with ourselves and our positions in the world, we learn to cope better and go on to different questions.

References

Adelson, J., Green, B., & O'Neil, R. Growth of the idea of law in adolescence. *Developmental Psychology*, 1969, *1*, 327–332.

Adelson, J., & O'Neil, R. The development of political thought in adolescence: A sense of community. *Journal of Personality and Social Psychology*, 1966, *4*, 295–308.

Allport, G. W. European and American theories of personality. In H. P. David & H. von Bracken (Eds.), *Perspectives in personality theory*. New York: Basic Books, 1957.

Arlin, P. K. Cognitive development in adulthood: A fifth stage? *Developmental Psychology*, 1975, *11*, 602–606.

Bakan, D. *The duality of human existence*. Chicago: Rand McNally, 1966.

Bakan, D. Adolescence in America: From idea to social fact. *Daedalus*, 1971.

Baldwin, C. P., & Baldwin, A. L. Children's judgments of kindness. *Child Development*, 1970, *41*, 29–47.

Becker, W. C. Consequences of different types of parental discipline. In M. L. Hoffman & L. W. Hoffman (Eds.), *Review of child development research* (Vol. 1). New York: Russell Sage, 1964. Pp. 169–208.

Beech, R. P., & Schoeppe, A. Development of value systems in adolescents. *Developmental Psychology*, 1974, *10*, 644–656.

Bem, S. The measurement of psychological androgyny. *Journal of Consulting and Clinical Psychology*, 1974, *42*, 155-162.

Bem, S. Sex-role adaptability: One consequence of psychological androgyny. *Journal of Personality and Social Psychology*, 1975, *31*, 634–643.

Benedict, R. Continuities and discontinuities in cultural conditioning. *Psychiatry*, 1938, *1*, 161–167.

Bernard, H. W. *Adolescent development*. Scranton, Penn.: Intext, 1971.

Black, A. Coordination of logical and moral reasoning in adolescence. Paper presented at the meeting of the Western Psychological Association, 1974.

Blasi, A., & Hoeffel, E. C. Adolescence and formal operations. *Human Development*, 1974, *17*, 344–363.

Block, J. Ego identity, role variability and adjustment. *Journal of Consulting Psychology*, 1961, *25*, 392–397.

Block, J., Von der Lippe, A., & Block, J. H. Sex role and socialization patterns:

Some personality concomitants and environmental antecedents. *Journal of Counsulting and Clinical Psychology*, 1973, *41*, 321–341.

Block, J. H. Conceptions of sex role: Some cross cultural and longitudinal perspectives. *American Psychologist*, 1973, *28*, 512–526.

Block, J. H., Haan, N., & Smith, M. B. Socialization correlates of student activism. *Journal of Social Issues*, 1969, *25*(4), 143–177.

Block, J. H., Haan, N., & Smith, M. B. Activism and apathy in contemporary adolescents. In J. F. Adams (Ed.), *Understanding adolescence*. Boston: Allyn & Bacon, 1973.

Borow, H. Career development in adolescence. In J. F. Adams (Ed.), *Understanding adolescence: Current developments in adolescent psychology*. Boston: Allyn & Bacon, 1973.

Bowles, S., & Wright, L. Personality integration in preadolescent males. Extended report of article appearing in *Developmental Psychology*, 1969, *2*, 151.

Brainerd, C. J. The development of the proportionality scheme in children and adolescents. *Developmental Psychology*, 1971, *5*, 469–476.

Brittain, C. V. Adolescent choices and parent-peer cross-pressures. *American Sociological Review*, 1963, *28*, 385–391.

Bronson, G. W. Identity diffusion in late adolescents. *Journal of Abnormal and Social Psychology*, 1959, *59*, 414–417.

Broverman, I. K., Vogel, S. R., Broverman, F. I., Clarkson, F. E., & Rosenkrantz, P. S. Sex-role stereotypes: A current appraisal. *Journal of Social Issues*, 1972, *28*, 56–78.

Bynum, T. W., Thomas, J. A., & Weitz, L. J. Truth functional logic in formal operational thinking. *Developmental Psychology*, 1972, *7*, 129–132.

Carlson, R. Stability and change in the adolescent's self-image. *Child Development*, 1965, *36*, 659–666.

Carlson, R. Sex differences in ego functioning: Exploratory studies of agency and communion. *Journal of Consulting and Clinical Psychology*, 1971, *37*, 267–277.

Chandler, M. J. Egocentrism and antisocial behavior: The assessment and training of social perspective-taking skills. *Developmental Psychology*, 1973, *9*, 326–332.

Chukovsky, K. *From two to five*. Berkeley: University of California Press, 1963.

Coleman, J. S. *The adolescent society*. Glencoe, Ill.: Free Press, 1961.

Coleman, J. S. Scholastic effects of the social system. In M. Gold & E. Douvan (Eds.), *Adolescent development*. Boston: Allyn & Bacon, 1969.

Coles, R. *Erik Erikson: The growth of his work*. Boston: Atlantic Monthly Press, 1970.

Constantinople, A. An Eriksonian measure of personality development in college students. *Developmental Psychology*, 1969, *1*, 357–372.

Constantinople, A. Some correlates of average level of happiness among college students. *Developmental Psychology*, 1970, *2*, 447.

Constanzo, P. R., & Shaw, M. E. Conformity as a function of age level. *Child Development*, 1966, *37*, 967–975.

Coons, F. W. The resolution of adolescence in college. *Personnel and Guidance Journal*, 1970, *48*, 533–541.

Cross, H. J., & Allen, J. G. Ego identity status, adjustment, and academic achievement. *Journal of Consulting and Clinical Psychology*, 1970, *34*, 228.

deJung, J. E., & Meyer, W. J. Expected reciprocity: Grade trends and correlates. *Child Development*, 1963, *34*, 127–139.

Derbyshire, R. L. Adolescent identity crisis in urban Mexican Americans in East Los Angeles. In E. B. Brody (Ed.), *Minority group adolescents in the United States.* Baltimore: Williams & Wilkins, 1968.

Dignan, M. H. Ego identity and maternal identification. *Journal of Personality and Social Psychology,* 1965, *1,* 476–483.

Douvan, E., & Adelson, J. *The adolescent experience.* New York: Wiley, 1966.

Dulit, E. Adolescent thinking á la Piaget: The formal stage. *Journal of Youth and Adolescence,* 1972, *1,* 281–301.

Dunphy, D. C. The social structure of urban adolescent peer groups. *Sociometry,* 1963, *26,* 230–246.

Dwyer, J., & Mayer, J. Psychological effects of variations in physical appearance during adolescence. *Adolescence,* 1968–69, *3,* 353–368.

Elkind, D. Quantity conceptions in junior and senior high school students. *Child Development,* 1961, *32,* 551–560.

Elkind, D. Quantity conceptions in college students. *Journal of Social Psychology,* 1962, *57,* 459–465.

Elkind, D. Conceptual orientation shifts in children and adolescents. *Child Development,* 1966, *37,* 493—498.

Elkind, D. Egocentrism in adolescence. *Child Development,* 1967, *38,* 1025–1034.

Elkind, D. *Children and adolescents: Interpretive essays on Jean Piaget.* New York: Oxford University Press, 1971.

Elkind, D., Barocas, R. B., & Johnsen, P. H. Concept production in children and adolescents. *Human Development,* 1969, *12,* 10–21.

Elkind, D., Barocas, R., & Rosenthal, B. Combinatorial thinking in adolescents from graded and ungraded classrooms. *Perceptual and Motor Skills,* 1968, *27,* 1015–1018.

Engel, M. The stability of the self-concept in adolescence. *Journal of Abnormal and Social Psychology,* 1959, *58,* 211–215.

Ennis, R. H. Children's ability to handle Piaget's propositional logic: A conceptual critique. *Review of Educational Research,* 1975, *45*(1), 1–41.

Erikson, E. The problem of ego identity. *Journal of the American Psychoanalytic Association,* 1956, *4,* 56–121.

Erikson, E. Youth and the life cycle. *Children,* March-April 1960, *7,* 43–49.

Erikson, E. *Identity: Youth and crisis.* New York: Norton, 1968.

Erikson, E. H. Youth: Fidelity and diversity. *Daedalus,* 1962, *91.*

Faust, M. S. Developmental maturity as a determinant in prestige of adolescent girls. *Child Development,* 1960, *31,* 173–184.

Feffer, M. H. The cognitive implications of role-taking behavior. *Journal of Personality,* 1959, *21,* 152–168.

Feinstein, S. C., & Ardon, M. S. Trends in dating patterns and adolescent development. *Journal of Youth and Adolescence,* 1973, *2,* 157–166.

Fendrich, J. M. Activists ten years later: A test of generational unit continuity. *Journal of Social Issues,* 1974, *30,* 95–118.

Field, T. W., & Cropley, A. J. Cognitive style and science achievement. *Journal of Research in Science Teaching,* 1969, *6,* 2–10.

Finger, J. A., Jr., & Silverman, M. Changes in academic performance in the junior high school. *Personnel and Guidance Journal,* 1966, *45,* 157–164.

Flavell, J. *The developmental psychology of Jean Piaget.* Princeton, N. J.: Van Nostrand, 1963.

Fleming, M., & Feinbloom, D. *Similarities in becoming: Transsexuals and adolescents.* Unpublished manuscript, Boston University, 1975.

Fontana, A. F., & Noel, B. Moral reasoning in the university. *Journal of Personality and Social Psychology*, 1973, *27*, 419–429.

Freides, D., Fredenthal, B. J., Grisell, J. L., & Cohen, B. D. Changes in two dimensions of cognition during adolescence. *Child Development*, 1963, *34*, 1047–1055.

Freud, A. *The ego and the mechanisms of defense.* New York: International Universities Press, 1966.

Furth, H. G. *Piaget for teachers.* Englewood Cliffs, N. J.: Prentice-Hall, 1970.

Gagnon, J. H., & Simon, W. *Sexual conduct.* Chicago: Aldine, 1973.

Galinsky, M. D. & Fast, I. Vocational choice as a focus of the identity search. *Journal of Counseling Psychology*, 1966, *13*, 89–92.

Gardner, H. *The quest for mind.* New York: Knopf, 1972.

Gilligan, C., Kohlberg, L., Lerner, J., & Belenky, M. Moral reasoning about sexual dilemmas. *Technical Report of the Commission on Obscenity and Pornography*, 1971, *1*, 141–174.

Ginsburg, H., & Opper, S. *Piaget's theory of intellectual development.* Englewood Cliffs, N. J.: Prentice-Hall, 1969.

Ginzberg, E. Toward a theory of occupational choice: A restatement. *Vocational Guidance Quarterly*, 1972, *20*, 169–176.

Glick, J., & Wapner, S. Development of transitivity: Some findings and problems of analysis. *Child Development*, 1968, *39*, 621–638.

Gold, M., & Douvan, E. *Adolescent development: Readings in research and theory.* Boston: Allyn & Bacon, 1969.

Goldman, R. J. The application of Piaget's scheme of operational thinking to religious story data by means of the Guttman scalogram. *British Journal of Educational Psychology*, 1965, *35*, 158–170.

Gollin, E. S. Organizational characteristic of social judgment: A developmental investigation. *Journal of Personality*, 1958, *26*, 139–154.

Goodnow, J. J. Test of milieu differences on some of Piaget's tasks. *Psychological Monographs*, 1962, *76*(36).

Gouin-Decarie, T. *Intelligence and affectivity in early childhood.* New York: International Universities Press, 1965.

Graves, A. J. Attainment of conservation of mass, weight, and volume in minimally educated adults. *Developmental Psychology*, 1972, *7*, 223.

Gray, S. W., & Klaus, R. A. The assessment of parental identification. Genetic Psychology Monographs, 1956, *54*, 81–114.

Group for the Advancement of Psychiatry. *Normal adolescence.* New York: Scribner's, 1968.

Gump, J. P. Sex role attitudes and psychological well being. *Journal of Social Issues*, 1972, *28*, 79–92.

Haan, N., Smith, M. D., & Block. J. H. Moral reasoning of young adults: Political-social behavior, family background, and personality correlates. *Journal of Personality and Social Psychology*, 1968, *10*, 183–201.

Hackman, R. D., & Davis, J. L. Vocational counseling with adolescents. In J. F. Adams (Ed.), *Understanding adolescence: Current developments in adolescent psychology.* Boston: Allyn & Bacon, 1973.

Halleck, S. L. Sex and mental health on the campus. *Journal of the American Medical Association*, 1967, *200*, 684–690.

Hamburg, B. A. Early adolescence: A specific and stressful stage of the life cycle. In G. V. Coello, D. A. Hamburg, & J. E. Adams (Eds.), *Coping and adaptation.* New York: Basic Books, 1974.

Hauck, B. B. Differences between the sexes at puberty. In E. D. Evans (Ed.), *Adolescents: Readings in behavior and development*. Hinsdale, Ill.: Dryden Press, 1970.

Hauser, S. T. Black and white identity formation: Aspects and perspectives. *Journal of Youth and Adolescence*, 1972, *1*, 113−130.

Havighurst, R. J. Youth in exploration and man emergent. In H. Borow (Ed.), *Man in a world at work*. Boston: Houghton Mifflin, 1964.

Heilbrun, A. B. An empirical test of the modeling theory of sex-role learning. *Child Development*, 1965, *36*, 789−799.

Higgins-Trenk, A., & Gaite, A. J. H. Elusiveness of formal operational thought in adolescents. *Proceedings of the 79th Annual Convention, American Psychological Association*, 1971, 108.

Hoffman, L. R. & Maier, N. R. F. Social factors influencing problem solving in women. *Journal of Personality and Social Psychology*, 1966, *4*, 382−390.

Hoffman, M. L. Conscience, personality and socialization techniques. *Human Development*, 1970, *13*, 90−126.

Hoffman, M. L. Father absence and conscience development. *Developmental Psychology*, 1971, *4*, 400−406. (a)

Hoffman, M. L. Identification and conscience development. *Child Development*, 1971, *42*, 1071−1082. (b)

Hoffman, M. L., & Salzstein, H. D. Parent discipline and the child's moral development. *Journal of Personality and Social Psychology*, 1967, *5*, 45−57.

Howard, M., & Kubis, J. F. Ego identity and some aspects of personal adjustment. *Journal of Psychology*, 1964, *58*(2), 459−466.

Hsu, F. L. K., Watrous, B. G., & Lord, E. M. Culture pattern and adolescent behavior. *International Journal of Social Psychiatry*, 1961, *7*, 33−53.

Inhelder, B., & Piaget, J. *The growth of logical thinking from childhood to adolescence*. New York: Basic Books, 1958.

Inhelder, B., & Piaget, J. *The early growth of logic in the child*. New York: Harper & Row, 1964.

Jackson, S. The growth of logical thinking in normal and subnormal children. *British Journal of Educational Psychology*, 1965, *35*, 255−258.

Johnson, M. Sex-role learning in the nuclear family. *Child Development*, 1963, *34*, 319−335.

Jones, M. C. The later careers of boys who were early- or late-maturing. *Child Development*, 1957, *28*, 113−128.

Jones, M. C. Psychological correlates of somatic development. *Child Development*, 1965, *36*, 899−911.

Jones, M. C., & Bayley, N. Physical maturing among boys as related to behavior. *Journal of Educational Psychology*, 1950, *41*, 129−148.

Jones, M. C., & Mussen, P. H. Self-conceptions, motivations and interpersonal attitudes of early- and late-maturing girls. *Child Development*, 1958, *29*, 491−501.

Josselyn, I. M. Sexual identity crises in the life cycle. In G. H. Seward & R. C. Williamson (Eds.), *Sex roles in changing society*. New York: Random House, 1970.

Kagan, J. Acquisition and significance of sex typing and sex role identity. In M. L. Hoffman & L. W. Hoffman (Eds.), *Review of child development research* (Vol. 1). New York: Russell Sage, 1964. Pp. 137−168.

Kagan, J. *Change and continuity in infancy*. New York: Wiley, 1971.

Kanin, E. J. An examination of sexual aggression as a response to sexual frustration. *Journal of Marriage and the Family*, 1967, *29*, 428–433.

Katz, P., & Zigler, E. Self-image disparity: A developmental approach. *Journal of Personality and Social Psychology*, 1967, *5*, 186–195.

Kinsey, A. C., Pomeroy, W. B., & Martin, C. E. *Sexual behavior in the human male*. Philadelphia: Saunders, 1948.

Klineberg, S. L. Changes in outlook on the future between childhood and adolescence. *Journal of Personality and Social Psychology*, 1967, *7*, 185–193.

Kohlberg, L. The development of children's orientations toward a moral order. *Vita Humana*, 1963, *6*, 11–33.

Kohlberg, L. Moral development and identification. In H. W. Stevenson (Ed.), *Child psychology, 62nd yearbook of the National Society for the Study of Education*. Chicago: University of Chicago Press, 1963.

Kohlberg, L. A cognitive developmental analysis of children's sex role concepts and attitudes. In E. Maccoby (Ed.), *The development of sex differences*. Stanford, Calif.: Stanford University Press, 1966.

Kohlberg, L. Continuities in childhood and adult moral development revisited. In P. B. Baltes & K. W. Schaie (Eds.), *Life-span developmental psychology: Personality and socialization*. New York: Academic Press, 1973.

Kohlberg, L., & Gilligan, C. The adolescent as a philosopher: The discovery of the self in a postconventional world. *Daedalus*, 1971, *100*, 1051–1086.

Kohlberg, L., & Kramer, R. Continuities and discontinuities in childhood and adult moral development. *Human Development*, 1969, *12*, 93–120.

Kuhlen, R. G., & Arnold, M. Age differences in religious beliefs and problems during adolescence. *Journal of Genetic Psychology*, 1944, *65*, 291–300.

Kuhn, D., Langer, J., Kohlberg, L., & Haan, N. *The development of formal operations in logical and moral judgment*. Unpublished manuscript, Harvard University, 1971.

L'Abaté, L. The status of adolescent psychology. *Developmental Psychology*, 1971, *4*, 201–205.

Lambert, B. G., Rothschild, B. F., Altland, R., & Green, J. B. *Adolescence: Transition from childhood to maturity*. Monterey, Calif.: Brooks/Cole, 1972.

Landsbaum, J. B., & Willis, R. H. Conformity in early and late adolescence. *Developmental Psychology*, 1971, *4*, 334–337.

Lee, L. C. The concomitant development of cognitive and moral modes of thought: A test of selected deductions from Piaget's theory. *Genetic Psychology Monographs*, 1971, *83*, 93–146.

Lefrancois, G. R. *Psychological theories and human learning: Kongor's report*. Monterey, Calif.: Brooks/Cole, 1972.

Lerner, S., Bie, I., & Lehrer, P. Concrete-operational thinking in mentally ill adolescents. *Merrill-Palmer Quarterly*, 1972, *18*, 287–291.

Lessing, E. E. Extension of personal future time perspective, age, and life satisfaction of children and adolescents. *Developmental Psychology*, 1972, *6*, 457–468.

Levenson, M., & Neuringer, C. Problem solving behavior in suicidal adolescents. *Journal of Consulting and Clinical Psychology*, 1971, *37*, 433–436.

Lewis, S. H., & Kraut, R. E. Correlates of student political activism and ideology. *Journal of Social Issues*, 1972, *28*, 131–149.

Lidz, T. Schizophrenic thinking. *Journal of Youth and Adolescence*, 1974, *3*, 95–98.

Loevinger, J. The meaning and measurement of ego development. *American Psychologist*, 1966, *21*, 195–206.

Lovell, K. *The growth of basic mathematical and scientific concepts in children.* New York: Philosophical Library, 1961.

Lunzer, E. A. *Recent studies in Britain based on the work of Jean Piaget.* London: National Foundation for Educational Research in England & Wales, 1960, *201*.

Lunzer, E. A. Problems of formal reasoning in test situations. *Monographs of the Society for Research in Child Development*, 1965, *30*(2), 19–46.

Lynn, D. B. The process of learning parental and sex-role identification. *Journal of Marriage and the Family*, 1966, *18*, 466–470.

Maccoby, E. E., & Jacklin, C. N. *The psychology of sex differences.* Stanford, Calif.: Stanford University Press, 1974.

Marcia, J. E. Development and validation of ego identity status. *Journal of Personality and Social Psychology*, 1966, *3*, 551–558.

Marcia, J. E. Ego identity status: Relationship to change in self-esteem, "general maladjustment," and authoritarianism. *Journal of Personality*, 1967, *35*, 118–134.

Marcia, J. E., & Friedman, M. L. Ego identity status in college women. *Journal of Personality*, 1970, *38*, 249–263.

McCandless, B. R. *Adolescents: Behavior and development.* Hinsdale, Ill.: Dryden, 1970.

McCreary-Juhasz, A. How accurate are student evaluations of the extent of their knowledge of human sexuality? *Journal of School Health*, 1967, *37*, 409–412.

McDonald, R. L., & Gynther, M. D. Relationship of self and ideal-self descriptions with sex, race and class in southern adolescents. *Journal of Personality and Social Psychology*, 1965, *1*, 85–88.

Mead, M. *Male and female.* New York: William Morrow, 1949.

Mead, M. Adolescence. In H. V. Kraemer (Ed.), *Youth and culture: A human-development approach.* Monterey, Calif.: Brooks/Cole, 1974.

Milton, G. A. Six differences in problem solving as a function of role appropriateness of the problem content. *Psychological Reports*, 1959, *5*, 705–708.

Money, J., & Ehrhardt, A:A. *Man and woman, boy and girl.* Baltimore: Johns Hopkins, 1972.

Moss, H. Sex, age, and state as determinants of mother-infant interaction. *Merrill-Palmer Quarterly*, 1967, *13*, 19–36.

Mullener, N., & Laird, J. D. Some developmental changes in the organization of self-evaluations. *Developmental Psychology*, 1971, *5*, 233–236.

Mussen, P. H., & Boutourline-Young, H. Relationships between rate of physical maturing and personality among boys of Italian descent. *Vita Humana*, 1964, *7*, 186–200.

Mussen, P. H., & Jones, M. C. Self-conceptions, motivations, and interpersonal attitudes of late- and early-maturing boys. *Child Development*, 1957, *28*, 243–256.

Muus, R. E. Adolescent development and the secular trend. *Adolescence*, 1970, *5*, 267–284.

Nachmann, B. Childhood experience and vocational choice in law, dentistry and social work. *Journal of Counseling Psychology*, 1960, *7*, 243–250.

Neimark, E. A. A preliminary search for the formal operations structures. *Journal of Genetic Psychology,* 1970, *116,* 223–232.

Neimark, E. D., & Lewis, N. Development of logical problem solving: A one-year retest. *Child Development,* 1968, *39,* 527–536.

Nevid, J., Nevid, A., O'Neill, M., & Waterman, C. K. Sex differences in resolution of sexual identity crisis. Paper presented at the Eastern Psychological Association meeting, 1974.

Offer, D. *The psychological world of the teen-ager.* New York: Basic Books, 1969.

Offer, D., & Offer, J. B. *From teenage to young manhood.* New York: Basic Books, 1975.

Orlofsky, J. L., Marcia, J. E., & Lesser, I. M. Ego identity status and the intimacy vs. isolation crisis of young adulthood. *Journal of Personal and Social Psychology,* 1973, *27,* 211–219.

Papalia, D. E. The status of several conservation abilities across the life-span. *Human Development,* 1972, *15,* 229–243.

Parsons, C. Inhelder and Piaget's "The Growth of Logical Thinking." II. A logician's viewpoint. *British Journal of Psychology,* 1960, *51,* 75–84.

Parsons, T. Social structure and the development of personality: Freud's contribution to the integration of psychology and sociology. *Psychiatry,* 1958, *21,* 321–340.

Payne, D. C. Sex education and the sexual education of adolescents. In E. D. Evans (Ed.), *Adolescents: Readings in behavior and development.* Hinsdale, Ill.: Dryden, 1970.

Peel, E. A. Intellectual growth during adolescence. *Educational Review,* 1965, *17,* 169–180.

Peel, E. A. *The nature of adolescent judgment.* New York: Wiley-Interscience, 1971.

Piaget, J. *The moral judgment of the child.* New York: The Free Press, 1965.

Piaget, J. *Six psychological studies.* New York: Vintage Books, 1968.

Piaget, J. The intellectual development of the adolescent. In G. Caplan & S. Lebovici (Eds.), *Adolescence: Psychosocial perspectives.* New York: Basic Books, 1969.

Piaget, J. Piaget's theory. In P. H. Mussen (Ed.), *Carmichael's manual of child psychology.* New York: Wiley, 1970.

Piaget, J. Intellectual evolution from adolescence to adulthood. *Human Development,* 1972, *15,* 1–12, 34.

Piers, E. V., & Harris, D. B. Age and other correlates of self-concept in children. *Journal of Educational Psychology,* 1965, *55,* 91–95.

Pleck, J. H. Masculinity-femininity: Current and alternate paradigms. *Sex Roles,* 1975, *1,* 161–178.

Podd, M. H. Ego identity status and morality: The relationship between two developmental constructs. *Developmental Psychology,* 1972, *6,* 497–507.

Rasmussen, J. E. The relationship of ego identity to psychosocial effectiveness. *Psychological Reports,* 1964, *15,* 815–825.

Rebelsky, F., & Speisman, J. C. Career education and liberal arts. *Science,* 1975, *188.*

Reiss, I. L. Social class and premarital sexual permissiveness: A reexamination. *American Sociological Review,* 1965, *30,* 747–757.

Reiss, I. L. The sexual renaissance: A summary and analysis. *Journal of Social Issues,* 1966, *22,* 123–137.

Reiss, I. L. How and why America's sex standards are changing. *Transaction*, 1968, *5*, 26—32.

Rheingold, H. L., & Cook, K. V. The content of boys' and girls' rooms as an index of parents' behavior. *Child Development*, 1975, *46*, 459—463.

Rosenberg, B., & Bensman, J. Sexual patterns in three ethnic subcultures of an American underclass. *Annals of the American Academy of Political and Social Sciences*, 1968, *376*, 61—75.

Schenkel, S. Relationship among ego identity status, field-independence and traditional femininity. *Journal of Youth and Adolescence*, 1975, *4*, 73—82.

Schenkel, S., & Marcia, J. E. Attitudes toward premarital intercourse in determining ego identity status in college women. *Journal of Personality*, 1972, *3*, 472—482.

Schimek, J. G. Cognitive style and defenses: A longitudinal study of intellectualization and field independence. *Journal of Abnormal Psychology*, 1968, *73*, 575—580.

Schonfeld, W. A. Adolescent development: Biological, psychological and sociological determinants. In S. C. Feinstein, P. L. Giovacchni, & A. A. Miller (Eds.), *Adolescent psychiatry* (Vol. 1). New York: Basic Books, 1971.

Seeman, J. Personality integration in college women. *Journal of Personality and Social Psychology*, 1966, *4*, 91—93.

Selman, R. L. The relation of role taking to the development of moral judgment in children. *Child Development*, 1971, *42*, 79—91.

Serban, G. The development of neurotic thinking. *Journal of Youth and Adolescence*, 1974, *3*, 99—104.

Serbin, L. A., O'Leary, K. D., Kent, R. N., & Tonick, I. J. A comparison of teacher responses to the pre-academic and problem behavior of boys and girls. *Child Development*, 1973, *44*, 796—804.

Shaffer, L. F. *Children's interpretations of cartoons*. New York: Teachers College Contributions to Education No. 429, 1930.

Siegler, R. S., Liebert, D. E., & Liebert, R. M. Inhelder and Piaget's pendulum problem: Teaching preadolescents to act as scientists. *Developmental Psychology*, 1973, *9*, 97—101.

Simon, W., Berger, A. S., & Gagnon, J. H. Beyond anxiety and fantasy: The coital experiences of college youth. *Journal of Youth and Adolescence*, 1972, *1*, 203—222.

Simpson, E. L. Moral development research: A case study of scientific cultural bias. Human Development, 1974, *17*, 81—106.

Spence, J. T., Helmreich, R., & Stapp, J. Ratings of self and peers on sex-role attributes and their relation to self-esteem and conceptions of masculinity and femininity. *Journal of Personality and Social Psychology*, 1975, *32*, 29—39.

Stephens, B. The development of reasoning, moral judgment, and moral conduct in retardates and normals. Phase II: Research Report, May, 1972, Division of Research and Demonstration Grants, Social and Rehabilitation Service, Department of HEW. (Research Report, May, 1972—Research Grant No. 15-P-5512113-02.)

Stephens, B., McLaughlin, J. A., Miller, C. K., & Glass, G. V. Factorial structure of selected psycho-educational measures and Piagetian reasoning assessments. *Developmental Psychology*, 1972, *6*, 343—348.

Tanner, J. M. *Growth at adolescence*. Springfield, Ill.: Charles C Thomas, 1962.

Tanner, J. M. Physical growth. In P. H. Mussen (Ed.), *Carmichael's manual of child psychology*, New York: John Wiley & Sons, 1970.

Tanner, J. M. Sequence, tempo, and individual variation in the growth and development of boys and girls aged 12 to 16. *Daedalus*, 1971.

Tapp, J., & Kohlberg, L. Developing senses of law and legal justice. *Journal of Social Issues*, 1971, *27*, 65–91.

Tapp, J. L., & Levine, F. J. Persuasion to virtue. *Law and Society Review*, 1970, 565–582.

Tapp, J. L., & Levine, F. J. Compliance from kindergarten to college: A speculative research note. *Journal of Youth and Adolescence*, 1972, *1*, 233–249.

Tasch, R. J. The role of the father in the family. *Journal of Experimental Education*, 1952, *20*, 319–361.

Thomas, L. E. Political generation gap: A study of liberal and conservative activist and nonactivist students and their parents. *Journal of Social Psychology*, 1971, *84*, 313–314.

Thompson, G. G., & Gardner, E. F. Adolescents' perceptions of happy-successful living. *Journal of Genetic Psychology*, 1969, *115*, 107–120.

Thornburg, H. D. (Ed.). *Contemporary adolescence: Readings*. Monterey, Calif.: Brooks/Cole, 1971.

Tisher, R. P. A Piagetian questionnaire applied to pupils in a secondary school. *Child Development*, 1971, *42*, 1633–1636.

Toder, N. L., & Marcia, J. E. Ego identity status and response to conformity pressure in college women. *Journal of Personality and Social Psychology*, 1973, *26*, 287–294.

Tomlinson-Keasey, C. Formal operations in sixth-graders, college coeds and 50-year old women. Extended report of brief article in *Developmental Psychology*, 1972, *6*, 364.

Tomlinson-Keasey, C., & Keasey, C. B. The mediating role of cognitive development in moral judgment. *Child Development*, 1974, *45*, 291–298.

Tracy, J. J., & Cross, H. J. Antecedents of shift in moral judgment. *Journal of Personality and Social Psychology*, 1973, *26*, 238–244.

Turiel, E. Conflict and transition in adolescent moral development. *Child Development*, 1974, *45*, 14–29.

Vaz, E. W. Delinquency and the youth culture: Upper and middle-class boys. *Journal of Criminal Law, Criminology, and Police Science*, 1969, *60*(1), 33–46.

Vetter, G. B., & Green, M. Personality and group factors in the making of atheists. *Journal of Abnormal and Social Psychology*, 1932, *27*, 179–194.

Voyat, G. I.Q.: God-given or man-made? *Saturday Review*, May 17, 1969, 73–75.

Wagner, N. N. Adolescent sexual behavior. In E. D. Evans (Ed.), *Adolescents: Readings in behavior and development*. Hinsdale, Ill.: Dryden, 1970.

Walberg, H. J. Physics, femininity, and creativity. *Developmental Psychology*, 1969, *1*, 47–54.

Wason, P. C., & Johnson-Laird, P. N. *Psychology of reasoning*. Cambridge, Mass.: Harvard University Press, 1972.

Waterman, A. S., Geary, P., & Waterman, C. A longitudinal study of changes in ego identity status from the freshman to the senior year at college. *Developmental Psychology*, 1974, *10*, 387–392.

Waterman, A. S., & Waterman, C. K. A longitudinal study of changes in ego identity status during the freshman year at college. *Developmental Psychology*, 1971, *5*, 167–173.

Waterman, A. S., & Waterman, C. K. Relationship between freshman ego identity status and subsequent academic behavior. A test of the predictive validity of Marcia's categorization system for identity status. *Developmental Psychology*, 1972, *6*, 179.

Waterman, C. K., & Waterman, A. S. Fathers and sons: A study of ego identity across two generations. *Journal of Youth and Adolescence*, 1975, *4*, 331–338.

Weatherley, D. Self-perceived rate of physical maturation and personality in late adolescence. *Child Development*, 1964, *35*, 1197–1210.

Webster, H. Changes in attitudes during college. *Journal of Educational Psychology*, 1958, *49*, 109–117.

Weiner, B., & Peter, N. A cognitive-developmental analysis of achievement and moral judgments. *Developmental Psychology*, 1973, *9*, 290–309.

Weitz, L. J., Bynum, T. W., Thomas, J. A., & Steger, J. A. Piaget's system of 16 binary operations: An empirical investigation. *Journal of Genetic Psychology*, in press.

White, K. M., & Friedman, B. Conservation of volume in college students: Refuting Elkind. *Journal of Genetic Psychology*, 1976, in press.

White, K. M., & Mervis, J. *Females and males: Who's logical and when?* Unpublished paper, Boston University, 1975.

Williams, R. L., & Byars, H. Negro self-esteem in a transitional society. *Personnel and Guidance Journal*, 1968, *47*, 120–125.

Wright, D., & Cox, E. A study of the relationship between moral judgment and religious belief in a sample of English adolescents. *Journal of Social Psychology*, 1967, *72*, 135–144.

Yarrow, L. J., Rubenstein, J. L., & Pedersen, F. A. Dimensions of early stimulation: Differential effects on infant development. Paper presented at the meeting of the Society for Research in Child Development, 1971. Cited in E. E. Maccoby & C. N. Jacklin, *The psychology of sex differences*. Stanford, Calif.: Stanford University Press, 1974.

Younnis, J., Furth, H. G., & Ross, B. M. Logical symbol use in deaf and hearing adolescents, 1973, *5*, 511–517.

Yudin, L., & Kates, S. L. Concept attainment and adolescent development. *Journal of Educational Psychology*, 1963, *54*, 177–182.

Author Index

Subject Index